Garden of the
Sufi

Garden of the Sufi

Insights into the Nature of Man

Jim D. Aghevli

Humanics Publishing
Atlanta, Georgia

Garden of the Sufi: Insights Into the Nature of Man
A Humanics Trade Publication

Humanics Trade Publications are an imprint of and published by Humanics Limited, a division of Humanics Publishing Group, Inc. Its trademark, consisting of a Pegasus, is registered in U.S. Patent and Trademark Office and in other countries.

Humanics Limited, P.O Box 7400, Atlanta, GA 30357

Library of Congress Cataloging-in-Publication Data

Aghevli, J.D.
Garden of the Sufi: Insights into the Nature of Man

1. Sufism 2. Religion—Philosophy
I. Title
CIP 98-85984
ISBN 0-89334-269-6

Illustrations and book design by Jessica Greene
Edited by Christopher Walker

Table of Contents

Dedication

To the name of the one who created thoughts,
brightened the light of hearts with the candle of life.
Enlightened both world with his thoughts;
his alms made this world a garden for mankind.
Shabestari

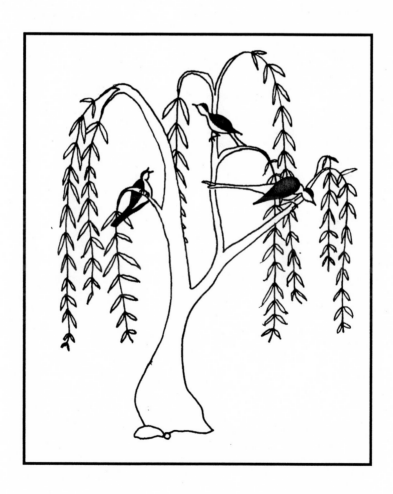

Preface

Never dies the one who was enlightened by Love
Our timelessness is written on the pages of time.
(Hafez, Ode 10, 3)

The bell toll of the church, the mantra of the Hindus, the call of the Muezzin, the meditation of Tibetan monks, the psalms of the Jews, the hymns of the Zoroastrians, the dance of the whirling dervishes: each with its own flavor and beauty represent our attempts to attain some higher understanding and a greater, more meaningful existence. This desire is a common theme throughout religions and cultures around the world. But we have stained the pages of history by producing the soldiers of bigotry, malice, and war, who entrapped our lofty visions within the walls of mundane fortresses. With the light of truth, we begin to chip away at these monstrous walls, seeking a better consciousness which we all know exists.

The mystical, spiritual and philosophical ways of the Sufi have such depth that they overwhelm whoever comes in contact with them. Unfortunately, during the past four centuries, the grand scale of this sacred and ancient way has ceased, and the movement has become devoid of the enthusiasm needed to carry its torch forward. However, although Sufism has waned, people throughout the world still have a desire to know about a philosophy that has such power and measurable answers to questions Western Civilization normally thinks of as subjective and ultimately relative to the situation.

In the early part of the twentieth century, academics in the Western hemisphere went beyond studying the Occidental writings and touched upon certain Sufi works. Accordingly, college students soon became interested in this subject. When my own children reached this age, they asked me to translate some of my favorite Sufi works for them. Touching the sacred *Thoughts of Beyond* required enormous effort, and for this I prayed for strength and the guiding light many times. My humble attempt to present an overview of this endless ocean of thought became this direct translation of selected works of the known Sufi masters of the eleventh to fifteen the centuries. This era, also referred to as the Golden Era, was very similar to the Renaissance period in Europe, as all the major Sufi works were written at during this time period.

This book is arranged to introduce the thoughts of the Sufi to a beginner, and to this end, each chapter should be read as recommended. The chapter "Tales of the Nightingale," consisting of an assortment of various philosophical poems presented to provide the mood to read the following chapters does not have to be read in one sitting. "Affliction in the Garden" contains two sections: "The Words of Ecstasy," which explains the metaphors used in the poetry, is a must-read section. The second section, "The Martyrs," a saga of two Sufi masters, can be read independently. The remaining chapters, "Seeds of the Flowers" describing the teachings and "Songs of Heavens" describing the mystical states, should be read straight through.

The reader will realize that the writings of the Sufi encompass and build on the foundations of the Koran and the Bible. Those who are familiar with these works should have no problem understanding the context. However, since the culture of the Zoroastrians has been interwoven with Iranian culture, I, at times, make references to some of the characters or stories mentioned in the Holy Avesta. I hope I have provided a proper presentation and like to cite the wishes of Hakiem Nezami, who wrote the following:

Prayer

O' Lord open the doors of success to me
guide me to the path of inquiry.
Grant me the heart to see your certainty,
the talent to adore your name of dignity.
Let no evil thoughts come in my heart;
stop my hand from reaching the wrong.
Enlighten my soul with your glow,
to praise you in my verses with heavenly flow.
Make my psalms reach the heavenly height;
with Spirit of David freshen my heart.
The nightingale I nourished with my soul,
with your blessing, show her to the world.
Give my verses the spell that enlightens,
the heavenly scent that mesmerizes;
make its scripts enlightening to eyes,
with melodies that entertain thoughts.
The spirit that brings liberty to hearts,
the way to the secrets, the key to locks.
Make its meaning, the essence of pride
the fashion causing fortune to abide.
The face with the beauty of Shirin's eyes,
a destiny, fitting her wavy tress with locks.
Aid me with the breeze of your helping sea;
donate a drop from your treasures to me.
Since the Giver is merciful and kind,
search the mystic labyrinth of your mind.
(Nezami, Book of Khosro and Shirin, Ode 1)

I like to thank the many individuals who enriched my work with their contribution regarding the Sufi thinking presented here. I would like to thank my late father Mohammad Ali Aghevli, a true Sufi at heart, the Assemblies of the Okhovat Sufi order of Tehran, Ahmad Kosha, Ghasem Ghani, Said Nafisy, Reynold Alleyne Nicholson, Ovaness Ovanessian, and many others whose names are all in my heart. Also, I would like to acknowledge the inspiration and encouragement I received from my wife Josephine and my children, who were deprived of a husband and father, but who patiently provided the environment for me to work on the arduous translations and organization of this work. They made this book possible.

Introduction

> To the name of the Holy, creator of life and thought,
> words cannot reach that plateau of height.
> *(Ferdousi, Book of Kings, 1)*

The call of the reed with the rhythms of the tambour and the dervishes' lamentations have echoed from the outskirts of China to Spain. The mystery of this call made Rumi start his *Mathnavi* with the following:

> Harken to the reed's plea in its cry,
> wails for separation, the time gone by.
> Since it was severed from its natal field,
> so many have cried to the sound of reed.
> *(Rumi, I, 1 & 2)*

Exactly when and where Sufi thought originated is a mystery. Some say that it is a child of Islam, but it seems more accurate to assume that Sufism developed along with the spread of Islam during the dark ages in Europe. Sufi themselves regard this question of beginning as irrelevant since they are more concerned with the present and the future than they are with the past.

While many people in the West believe that Sufism is merely a sect of Islamic beliefs, Sufi view themselves as a separate and higher religion. Sufi believe that all religion has a common theme: it is the thread which runs through each of the world's religions. One could claim that Sufism is not a religion but a stage of spiritual development and elevation that a true believer from any religion could attain, and since this is the true purpose of any religion, one can understand why Sufism has such universal appeal. Some researchers claim that Sufism must be the child of the Old Magi who had adopted an Islamic cloak. Nafisy, an eminent scholar on this subject, holds that Sufism is a blend of old and the new ideas, and that it must have originated somewhere in the area of Old Persia and moved westward through other parts of the new Islamic areas. Nafisy distinguishes three groups among the Sufi: The Persian-Indian Sufi, who blend Islamic and Buddhist beliefs, and two Arabic Sufi groups, one that blends Islamic and Gnostic beliefs, and another that holds Islamic and Judaic-Christian beliefs.

Sufism comprises a vast body of thought. In this book, I have limited myself to the works of the Sufi writers who originate from old Persia and its eastern steppes after the rise of Islam. Around the eighth century, Ibrahim ebn Adham Balkhi (d. 780), Abu Ali Shaghigh Blakhi (d. 790), and Hatam Assam (d. 851) distinguished themselves as the early and great Sufi masters. Soon thereafter Sufism suffered a hard setback at the hands of Ghengis and his great grandson Huluko Khan. Huluko Khan attacked from the east and the Islamic empires, badly crippled from the devastating crusades, crumbled. Word of mouth kept the wisdom of the early Sufi masters alive and their stories were eventually written down by later Sufi followers.

Finally, I would like to comment on the nature of my translation. It seems that a proper translation has to maintain the ambiguity contained in the original text. Only then, it seems to me, the reader is able to understand the text as it was intended and, at the same time, is encouraged to expand his own thoughts on the subject.

A proper translation should convey not only the exact meaning of the original text, it should also produce the same spirit. When translating poetry, however, reproducing rhymes and rhythms from a another language may prove a rather difficult endeavor. An exact translation requires adherence to a certain equivalent wording which may or may not provide the rhyme and the desired rhythm. Also, direct translations of certain metaphors could produce awkward phrases requiring lengthy English explanations. To avoid either of these problems, I have made some compromises in my translations.

To provide an accessible text, I have phonetically reproduced the Persian pronunciation of words to produce its English equivalent. Since pronunciation takes precedent over spelling, no special transliteration is used which would require devising additional letters. For the three Persian consonant sounds that do not have equivalents in English "a'," "gh," and "kh" are used. "A'" represents a strong and accented "a," "gh" represents a hard "g," and "kh" indicates a hard "k."

List of Sufi

Oryan-Baba Taher Hamedani was born in Hamedan. Locals called him Saint Khez. He appears in visions and dreams to direct the deserving people to the path of Sufi. Oryan is well known for his *Rubayyat* written in the local dialect, the language during the time of Sassanids.

Khayyam was born in Neyshabur and died in the same city circa 1142. Abdul Fateh Omar son of Ibrahim Neyshaburi, known as Khayyam the tent maker, became known originally as a mathematician and astronomer. Although Khayyam was not a Sufi, I have included him because of his philosophical insights in *Rubayyat.*

Attar (1155-1231). Fraidu'ddin Attar Neyshaburi was born in Neyshabur and died at the hand of one of Genghis Khan's soldiers during the invasion of that city. Rumi acknowledged Attar's talent. "Attar traversed the seven cities of love, where we are negotiating the bend of the first street." Attar became a Sufi after a follower once entered Attar's successful pharmacy and presented Attar with an extraordinary display of his will.

Nezami (1142-1205). Elias ebn Usuf known as Nezami Ganjavi was born in Ganje. Nezami is best known for his "Khosro o Shirin (K.S.)," a story of a Sassani King who fell in love with an Armenian Princess, Shirin, and "Layli o Majnuin (L.M.)," a story of two Arabian young lovers, similar to Shakespeare's *Romeo and Juliet.* Nezami relates the quest for the union of lovers to the desire to unite with the Lord.

Rumi (1207-1273). Molana Jalalu'ddin Mohammad ebn Husain, Balkhi, Khorasani known as Rumi was born in Balkh, now in Afghanistan. During Rumi's childhood, his family moved to Baghdad and later to Konya, now in Turkey. His father worked as a professor and Rumi took this position after his father's death. Influenced by his father and Attar, Rumi became familiar with the Sufi ideas and furthered his studies under Burhanu'ddin Mohaghegh Tormidi. Burhan and young Rumi traveled to Damascus and met with Ebn Arabi.

Later, under the teaching of Shams e Tabrizi, Rumi was transformed to a poet in a trance of live. The rhythmic hammering from a metal plant appeared to him as heavenly music and would cause him to go into a trance and compose poems. Rumi's poems are recorded in *Divan e Shams e Tabrizi*, (D.S.T.) and consist of nearly 35000 verses.

After the death of Shams, one of Rumi's students suggested to compose a book of *Mathnavi* in the same style that was developed by Attar and Sana'i. In an instant, Rumi took a piece of paper and wrote the first lines of *Mathnavi*, now a work of six volumes containing nearly 26000 verses.

Rumi wrote a total of 146 books. Most of them are now published either in Tehran or Istanbul. Some of Rumi's works have been translated into English by Reynold A. Nicholson in the 1930's. In this book, I have referred to the *Mathnavi* with its volume number as *Rumi, II,* followed by the number of the first line. Those gathered by Nicholson and others are referred to as *Rumi, M,* followed by the page number and the number of the first line. The *Divan e Shams e Tabrizi* is abbreviated as Rumi, D.S.T. followed by the number of the first line.

Sa'di Shirzai (1216-1293). Moshrefu'ddin Mosleh ebn Abdulah Sa'di Shirazi was born and educated in Shiarz and later studied in Baghdad under two teachers, who held opposing views regarding the Sufi. One of his teachers was Shahabu'ddin Sohrverdi (d. 1235), the author of *The Knowledge of Gnostic*, which discusses the origins, principles, and differences in various Sufi orders. Sa'di's other teacher was Abualfaraj ebn Josy (d. 1239) who wrote *Satan's Ruse* and considered the Sufis renegades. Sa'di traveled and studied until the age of forty when he began to write *Golestan* and *Bostan*, which are the names of the two gardens of paradise. Both are considered masterpieces in Persian literature.

Shabestari (1288-1339). Sa'du'ddin Mahmud ebn Aminu'ddin Shabestari studied under Aminu'ddin Baleh and Baha Ya'ghub Tabrizi. He originally lived in Shabestar but moved later to Kerman. Shabestari considered himself as a travelling Gnostic. He spent many years traveling through Arabia, Syria, and Egypt. During this time, Sufi poetry had gained much popularity. At the request of Amir Sid Husain Husini, Shabestari provided the answers to the seventeen frequently asked questions about "The Words of Ecstasy."

Hafez (1335-1388). Shamsu'ddin Mohammad e Shirazi was born and died in Shiraz. He was one of the most celebrated writers of his century. His ability to write and express his views in poetry remains unequaled. Hafez was known to have memorized the entire Koran and thus was given the name of Hafez, the keeper. He was inspired by Shah Nematu'Alah Vali, a known Sufi master.

Section I:
Tales of Nightingales

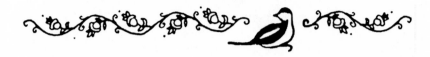

Some works of the best Sufi writers such as Attar, Rumi, Shabestrai, and Hafez are presented here to introduce the reader to Sufi philosophy and understanding. Because of the difficult nature of these writings, I have provided a brief explanation of the thoughts and concepts contained in each work.

The Beginning
It began with the C'morgh's amazing flight
in the sky of China in the midst of night.
From him a feather fell to the ground
and caused great excitement all around.
The colors and designs of the feather
caused all who saw it to become believers.
Now the feather lives in the land of design,
which inspires our desire for the Divine.
If the lines on the feather did not appear,
how could we have this excitement here?
Many messages come to us by his majesty,
as the design that excited our fantasies.
Alas, lacking the lines of the head and the tail,
of worthy tales for you, there are few to tell.
(Attar, M.T., 736)

C'mrogh is a large, legendary bird with special, god-given powers. C'morgh is part of ancient Iranian literature as well as folklore. In excerpts from the Holy Avesta, Nariman, the Persian champion, leaves his albino infant in the mountains to be eaten by wild birds. But C'morgh raises Saam, who later becomes Persia's champion and fathers another legendary bird, Rostam. C'morgh becomes a mentor for Saam and his family. Later C'morgh heals Rostam's wounds and guides him to victory over the invincible Esfandiar.

Attar's poem describes the origins of Sufism. C'morgh's feather is an example for the spiritual insights of the Sufis. Attar employs the feather as a visible sign for the knowledge and spiritual insights that Sufi have daily, but which the rest of us never even glimpse. The line, "If the lines on the feather did not appear, how could we have this excitement here?" refers to the draw of Sufism and its heightened spiritual awareness and consciousness.

Our Past Places

A man who lives for a while in a town
when he closes his eyes and lays down,
he may dream he is from another town,
but other memories do not come to his mind.
He would think he is from this town;
raised in another home, played on its lawn.
He wonders, does the soul not remember its past
the places it stayed and the abodes it had.
It doesn't remember that this world is a dream,
that covers the past with cloudy streams .
The soul has traveled through many towns;
the memory is dull but the dust is not yet gone.
(Rumi, IV, 3628)

Rumi states that as long as we dwell in the material world, we do not realize that it is a temporary world and a world of dreams. He indicates that in the temporary world man is separated from the Lord, but in the end he will return to the Lord. In this poem, the places indicate the experiences that the soul will gain during the time of its descent from the Lord to its reascension to divinity.

Leap of the Souls

I died as a rock and became a plant with a name;
as a plant I died and an animal I became.
I died as an animal and was born as a man;
why should I fear death, since from it I gain.
Next in my venture as a man I will die;
to soar as an angel, who is able to fly.
From angel-hood, a higher level I seek;
since all must perish except Him.
Again from angel-hood I will leap
to higher levels that we cannot conceive.
Then like a violet I shall vanish to naught;
until my return to Him, cease I will not.
(Rumi, III, 3901)

Rumi refers to the Sufi belief of coming from and ultimately returning to the Lord. It is interesting to note that Rumi here discusses reincarnation.

The Music from the Heavens

"T's said, the pipe and lute that charm our ears
derive their melody from rolling spheres;
But faith o'erpassing speculation's bound,
Can see what sweetens every jangled sound.
We, who are parts of Adam, heard with him
The song of Angels and of seraphim.
Our memory, though dull and sad, retains
Some echo still of those unearthly strains.
Oh, music is the meat of all who love,
Music uplifts the soul to realms above.
The ashes glow, the latent fires increase:
We who listen are fed with joy and peace."
(Rumi, IV, 734)

Akhavan Alsafai Basri in *Resaleh* states, "since the heavenly spheres and stars came to their orbits, the musical melodies also came into being; thus, music worships the Lord and makes the souls as well as the angels happy and excited and forget their sadness. This music is a reflection of the heavenly music...(206)." Hence, the Sufi consider music to be one of the means to reach higher levels.

Children of Light

There are stars beyond the stars,
free of combustion and sinister thoughts.
Other spheres with revolving orbs of their own;
not of the seven skies which to us are known.
The Lord's glow to imminent stars
comes unconnected but not apart
Whoever receives this glow of truth,
removes all disbelieving thoughts.
The anger of Mercury is not His
so with might be humble to please.
A glow invincible to the malice of dark,
passes between the fingers of God.
The enlightened, with blessed souls,
openly harvest this heavenly glow.
The one who sees this radiant Light
turns away from all but God.
Water flowing from sea to sea,
seeks always to return to its original sea.
From mountains rush the seeking streams
From bodies rush the loving souls.
(Rumi, I, 754)

The glow of the Lord comes from the world of beyond, a world free of worldly matters. It is a morally sober world, void of "sinister thoughts." In some references "combustion" (ehteragh) refers to the constellation of the Sun, Mercury, Jupiter, Mars, Venus, and Saturn as they pass at the same point on the orbit of the zodiac. "Combustion" may also represent chemical reactions.

Sufis believe that the world's affairs are controled by the heavenly bodies. The stars represent the traits of the Lord and affect the lives and the fates of the living.

Purpose of Creation

The reason for creating this world,
is to manifest what was to be known.
He created to show what He knew;
placing no parturition and throe.
You are unable to stay idle a while,
until your essence is revealed in time.
The struggle and the work you seek with zeal,
serve the purpose of your essence to reveal.
Your body is a reel that cannot rest,
since the brain continually pulls its thread.
Both worlds are in parturition and throes;
the cause, the mother; the effect, the birth of a child.
As the effect is born, it too becomes a cause,
And itself repeats the wondrous birth of a child.
Generations repeat this cause and effect;
Only enlightened eyes see this chain of events.
(Rumi, II, 994)

The constant struggle, i.e., the painful process of giving birth, perpetuates creation until all beings are manifested. It makes us aware of what the Lord has placed in this world.

Traveling Alone

Approved in our religion is glory, and strife
approved in Jesus is the ascetic life.
Traditions with crowds are best, O' friend
roads with no friends come to a sad end.
Evils and zeal you find on the road of faith;
the way of any epicene is not always with gem.
The test of religion is feared by man,
since it separates the seed from the bran.
Although you escape the wolf with your cautious ways,
no enjoyment comes without friends.
The mule, by nature with a company of friends,
comes to joy and will gain strength.
But alone, he must be lashed and lashed again
as he treads the way suffering in pain.
At least follow the logic of the mule;
do not travel alone, unless you are a fool.
(Rumi, VI, 494)

The first two lines of this poem refer to early Christians who chose to lead ascetic lives. Some early Moslems and Sufi followed their example. Many Sufi orders expanded on the idea of brotherhood as a way of life, a practice which is recommended by the Islamic faith and practiced by Christian monks throughout the world.

Grief of the Dead

What our Champion said is so true
from this world, whoever passes through,
has sorrow-not the sorrow of death;
but of missing the chance of killing the self.
He says: why did I not make this death my aim,
the way to eternal riches is lost, and I am to blame.
I based my aims on my blurry sight
and fixed my efforts on vanishing thoughts.
The grief of the dead is not from their death,
but from missing the chance to open the gate.
Having never perceived the dance of bubbles on the
sea,
I never understood why they came to shore to feed.
As waves throw the bubbles to the ground,
take some and tell them to look around.
Ask them, where is your swirl and zeal,
where is the movement you had in the sea?
Their words of silence will tell thee,
ask this not from us but from the sea.
How could bubbles move without waves,
how could dust be blown away.
If you see the dust, the wind you should also see;
you see bubbles, and also the force of the sea.
With careful looks you gain the insight to see;
do not gaze long at webs, bran, or lees.
Then beyond bodies you will gain sight
and follow your insight of all insights.
One look discerns only a yard or two of the road;
with repeated looks you will see the way of the Lord.
(Rumi, VI, 1450)

Rumi explains that the Lord is the cause of the events of the world. The answers provided by the foam "to ask the sea," have the same meaning: humans are "bubbles" and the Lord is the "sea."

Killing the "self" or becoming "naught" is one of the stages that the Sufi must reach through specific tasks which will be discussed later in this book and should not be understood as suicide.

The Hidden Power

We are harps waiting for you to strum;
when you touch the strings, your name we hum.
We are flutes with melodies from your blow,
we are the mountain; your voice we will echo.
We are the pieces of chess, making an advance,
but our victory and defeat are in your hands.
We are lions, but the kind on flags;
prevailing winds determine our attacks.
(Rumi, 1, 599)

Lions were one of the prevalent designs on flags. Lions are found on the flag of the Saljugh dynasty, for example. Rumi uses the lion metaphor to describe the relationship between humans and the Lord.

The Temporal Senses

Make your ears hear no sound;
close your eyes, and become blind.
Free your lower senses to this world,
then hearken to the message of the Lord.
Our thoughts and deeds are of the dusty road;
our inner journey is on the way of the Lord.
our dust born senses, dust will see;
while the spirit of Jesus walks on the sea.
(Rumi, I, 566)

The Sufi believe that the only way we can connect with the world of the beyond (referred to in some writings and this book as the "Truth") is through our six senses, or intuitions not by using a scientific, philosophical, or logical approach.

The Faces of Death

He who saw it as Joseph, ransomed his life,
or lost his faith, as did the seers of the brute wolf. (6)
The death of each person resembles his traits;
to a foe is a foe, to a friend is a friend.
You see your own color in mirrors;
deep to Africans, lighter to Turks.
You who run away in fear from death,
are scaring death from yourself.
The brute is yours and not the death's;
your life is a tree and its fruit is death.
If sweet or bitter, it is from your deeds.
The pain is from the thistles of your seed,
your comfort from silk is from your spin.
Deeds are not equal to their yields.
One passing the other is a lasting pith.
The laborer's work is unequal to his wage;
laboring is not proportional to its pay.
One is the effort of pain and sweat;
the other is of goods, gold, or silver.
But reward the faithful who worship and pray;
they will be in heaven in the garden of the blessed.
(Rumi, III, 3438)

Death, whether physically or spiritually, occurs in a fashion that reflects the personality of the person who is dying, i.e., a person with a pleasant personality will fall in love with death but a miser will run away from death to accumulate more wealth. Moreover, our deeds, although they seem to be stemming from our own free will, are predestined.

Praying for Discipline

Let us beseech God to help us with self control
or we are deprived from the blessing of the Lord.
To you if the gloom of sorrow befalls,
it arises from your irreverence, insolence, and faults.
The insolent man in the path of the Friend,
is not a good man, but a thief or brigand.
It was discipline that brought the world to light
and gave the angels their immaculate flight.
The dark of the eclipse is from our insolence;
the rejection of Izazil was from his irreverence.
(Rumi, I, 78)

In Sufism self-control is attained by learning to refrain from certain desires that are considered inappropriate by the faith. "Man" here means a person who has brought his desires under control and has acquired the necessary knowledge and understanding.

An "eclipse" is a reminder from the Lord of our undesirable deeds. Although it is scientifically understood that these events occur at predictable intervals, perhaps these intervals are divinely timed. The name "Izazil," in the last line, refers to Satan's original name.

Hope and Risk

As your cargo is placed on a boat,
you leave your fortune to hope.
Unaware you are of the end result;
whether the ship will be safe or with fault.
But if you venture only where you are sure,
there will be no adventures in life for you.
Then you are unfit to be a merchant;
for the outcome of a venture is always a secret.
The careful merchant with the heart of glass,
will never experience a gain or a loss.
Perhaps the one who loses is deprived;
but the loser with zeal will see the light.
Since the result of our work is our fate,
seek your salvation through the faith.
(Rumi, III, 3083)

Rumi explains that we do not know our destiny. At times we will succeed and at other times we will fail but all our efforts are orchestrated to fulfill the divine plans. Hence, the Sufi will not be angered by worldly affairs although the state of the world may not be pleasing to him. Further, Rumi suggests that a person who does not attempt anything because he fears failure or the unknown will never know pleasures that await those who try new things. Rumi's poem speaks somewhat to the familiar phrase, "Nothing ventured, nothing gained."

Sleep of the World

The emancipated soul from the body each night
erases memories from the tablets of the mind.
The soul travels away from its cage;
 free from orders, talks, and tales.
Prisoners will forget where they are,
rulers will forget their fiat and all.
No anxiety for profit and loss,
no plans for workers by their boss.
The Sufi has such state without sleep,
say "deem them awake while they are asleep."
Away from affairs of the day and night,
as the Lord's pen writing our fiat.
A silhouette was shown to those who seek,
while others were stolen away by sleep.
Their souls and bodies have no bounds;
in ease and peace they remain beyond.
Unless a messenger lays out bait,
 for the judgement calls their names.
As Seraphiel at the dawn of the day,
bids them to come forth from far away;
the detached souls will be confined again,
and their bodies will be laden again.
(Rumi, I, 388)

Ladder to the Heavens

The key to business success is your earthly traits;
to the ladder of the heavens is the senses in faith.
See an expert for the well of your traits,
beg the Beloved for the senses of faith.
The well of traits needs the body's health
to enrich the religious senses, and kill the self.
Ill comes to the body on the path of love,
then health prevails by thoughts of above.
He destroyed the house to find the gold;
then with the gold, the house was restored.
He stopped the flow and cleaned the ravine;
Then the flowing water became suitable to drink.
He cut the skin and removed the dart;
then new skin covered and healed the cut.
 He captured the castle from the pagans, destroyed;
with righteous construction, the castle was restored.
If the logic of these actions cannot be explained,
This short explanation was not free of pain.
At times he builds and at times he destroys;
uncertainties are inherent in religious work.
(Rumi, I, 303)

"Beloved" is a name the Sufi uses for the Lord. In many writings Sufism is sometimes referred to as "the path of love," or "the religion of love." Rumi's poem indicates that our mind cannot understand the reasoning behind many events we experience. Only "the gold," the soul, which is lives in "the house," our bodies, can "understand" seemingly illogical events.

Rewards of the Faithful

The faithful will say on the judgement day
O Angels, was not Hell on our way?
Through it infidels and faithful will walk,
but we saw no place of fires and flames.
The Angel smilingly will then reply,
the garden you saw with your eyes,
truly was Hell, for punishment hard,
but for you became a garden with shades,
became pleasant for your right deeds.
For God's sake the fire of lust in you was killed.
You calmed the anger with its burning flames,
remedied ignorance by joining the faith.
The fire of selfishness became a pleasant place,
as you planted the flowers of faith,
the place of rosary, nightingales of pray
chanting along the streams in heavenly shade.
Your deeds changed our burning Hell
to a heavenly place with riches of no end.
(Rumi, II, 2554)

Teaching from the Past

The nightingale on a tree top branch
sang in Pahlavi teaching of the past,
said: The fire of Moses is getting hot.
The message of the Lord is on the tree top.
The birds in garden are singing lyric with rhymes,
so long the master drinks to the Pahlavi songs.
In poverty we gained time of serene and leisure,
impossible to gain this with Kingly treasures.
Jamshied took only the tales of challis from the world.
If you set your heart in the worldly treasures, behold.
Hear the bizarre tales of the unfortunate,
the breath of Jesus killed them as a friend.
Destruction came to homes by playful ogling of thine;
 no need for more wine, in ecstasy your work is fine.
The wise baron nicely said to his son,
harvest only from your own crop.
O' Maiden did Hafez have too much wine?
it is falling down, this turban of mine.
(Hafez, Ode # 483)

The bird explains the old teaching in *Pahlavi*, the Persian language of the second through the seventh centuries A.D. The birds continue to sing in *Pahlavi* as long as the master drinks the wine. The followers are happy as long as the Sufi master is in trance and receives the words of the Lord.

Jamshied was an Avestic king, comparable to king Solomon in the Zoroastrian faith. Jamshied, with his strong ties to the deity, taught his people many traits and became very powerful. He owned a *challis* in which one could see the secrets of the world. His position made him very proud of himself. Eventually, his pride let him to believe he had become God's equal, a belief that cost him his life. However, the glorious Jamshied left us the stories of his *challis*.

Union of Souls

Faithful are many but the faith is one,
residing in different bodies but the soul is one.
Animals have spirit, brain and a role;
man reasoning, another purpose and a soul.
Besides to what was given to an ordinary man,
more was given to Saints by His hand.
The spirit of animals is for life;
toward union they will not strife.
As one excels, the others will not gain;
if one is laden, the others will feel no pain.
But one will rejoice to see the others dead;
or dies of envy to see the others with bread.
The souls of dogs are apart from wolves';
but in union is the souls of the Lions of Truth.
I used the plural form of this singular word,
to show its size in relations to its court,
just as the glow of the sun to a bungalow,
in relation to total of the sun's glow.
Each received light from one source,
see the light if no walls surrounded the courts.
But these bungalows have a vanishing role,
see eternity in union of the faithful' souls.
(Rumi, IV, 408-418)

Only the faithful, those who believe in the truth which originated from the Lord, will accomplish a true union of souls.

The Absolute Being

We are the pieces of chess checking to mate;
but the fate is from your graceful traits.
The life of life is you, who are we to say,
to enter in talks and sit to stay.
We appear to exist, but we are in naught
you are the being, in disguise you are not.
We are the lions, but the kind on flags;
the prevailing wind determines our attacks.
Their attack is apparent but not the wind;
hope we are not forsaken by the Unseen.
Our lives and being are from your gift,
from your cessation we came to exist.
The ecstasy of being you created for naught;
you to yourself made us to fall in love.
Do not take away the ecstasy of your alms,
do not take away the sweets and the wine.
If you take away these, who will be your seekers;
the paintings cannot demand from painters.
Do not look to us nor expect from us much;
look to your graceful kindness of your touch.
We had no demands when we were in naught;
but your grace in silence was hearing our wants.
In his of audience the helpless creatures,
are the tapestries facing the needles.
Next, may sew the shape of a devil or a man,
next may sew a happy scenery or one of sad.
No hand can be raised in our defense;
no voice will speak for our welfares.
(Rumi, I, 602)

The soul is the moving force of the body as the wind moves the flags and the design on it, i.e., the shape of a lion. When we were separated from the Lord and came to our temporal beings, our love for the Lord came with us. Our helplessness regarding the desires of the Lord are like the flag Rumi describes in the poem.

The Phenomenal Bridge

As Christian goes to a priest to confess,
of fornication, hypocrisy or malice,
asks the priest to pardon of his sins,
the priest pardon is of the Lord in his beliefs.
The priest is uncertain of the Lord's deeds,
but works like magic our love and beliefs.
In absence, many designs were inspired by love,
cast many spells to reach the above.
Says: I am the awareness and the trance,
the beauties in designs are from my essence.
Since to my reflections, for long, you gazed,
now to my audience you may attend.
As the yonder pulls, the Christian feels,
now, he sees no church, no priests in between.
Then he asks for the forgiveness for his sins,
reaches the Lord's grace, while on his knees
through rocks, water emerges from below
then the rocks become inundated by the flow.
(Rumi, V, 3257 & 3280)

Faith creates a bridge between the confessor and the Lord. A confession with love and faith becomes more truthful and profound.

The Mother's Affliction

As a mother in affliction with a heavy heart,
stands at the grave of her newly dead child,
talks of many secrets, endeavors and divine;
she imagines her child is not dead but alive.
not present but alive, is the dust,
living ears are the surrounding brush.
To her each speckle of the dust of the grave,
has the brain and understands her pain.
She talks as though the dust is alive;
look at the amazing work of love.
To the fresh smelling dirt of the grave,
she pours her lamenting, sincere tears.
But in the time when the child was alive,
not so much love was shown in his life.
As her afflictions is pacified by time,
the blaze of her love will calm down.
The love for the dead if not of the last kind;
love the life of those who enrich lives.
Soon sleep will steal her away from dust;
the dust will bear her only dust.
As love departs will take away its spells,
only ash remains in the place of the blaze .
(Rumi, V, 3265)

Does motherly love pull her towards eternity? After the child is buried, the mother realizes that its soul is the only part that remains "valuable." The body is earthly and has little or no "value." Hence, the Sufi do not believe in erecting tombstones for their deceased.

The True Light

Lanterns, bulbs, wicks are diverse,
but the emitting lights of beyond, are the same.
If your eyes are focused on the glass, you will be lost,
from the dichotomy that comes to your sight.
You will be overwhelmed if you focus on the light
which takes you beyond the dichotomy of sight.
Our logic is from our dichotomous point of view:
the discord of the Pagans, Moslems and Jews.
(Rumi, III, 1255)

The shapes and the glass refer to earthly beings. The light is the soul which comes from beyond.

Differing Views

An elephant was placed in a room for show
in a dark room receiving no light nor glow.
The elephant was impossible to see,
the shape could be determined only by feel.
The one who touched the trunk said:
it is round and long like a conduit.
The one who touched the ear,
said: wide and thin as a fan, nothing to fear.
The one who touched the leg,
said it is round and thick like a peg.
Did say the one who touched the back
it is flat and smooth a place to relax.
But if one had brought a candle inside,
could have found the shape with sight.
(Rumi, III, 1259)

Although each person who touched a part of the elephant correctly described what he felt, no one could describe the elephant in totality. This experiment alludes to the various religious belief systems around the world. Each faith holds its own view of the Truth, and each in its own possesses a part of it.

The Written and the Intended

Know not the words of Koran as written
for under the written are meanings hidden.
Under the second is another meaning anew,
which dazes the thoughts and views.
The fourth, except the Prophet, none had seen;
the glory of God, the Unequal Unseen.
Count such hidden meanings to seven;
amazing intent stories of heavens.
O' friend, do not look at the cover of Koran;
man appears only as piece of meat to Satan.
Like a human being is the holy Koran
a shape for outside with a soul quietly inside.
(Rumi, M. III, 4244)

Rumi advises that to understand the writings of the Holy Koran properly ordinary people cannot accept its words exactly as they appear on the page and expect to receive the true word of the Lord. Only prophets can interpret the Holy Koran.

Love of a Woman

You rule the woman only seemingly,
but, you yearn and obey her eagerly.
Such is the character of man;
animals with less love, lack.
The Prophet said that women
rule the good hearted men.
but women are ruled by brutes,
with animal instinct so cruel.
Human quality is kindness and love;
the animal quality is anger and lust.
woman is the ray of God, the beloved;
as though she is the creator and not the created.
(Rumi, 1, 2431)

A woman, the most beautiful creature on earth in the eye of a man, represents a part of the beauty of the Lord. However, her earthly beauty cannot be compared with eternal beauty.

The following passages are one story and the explanations for all three parts are provided at the end of the third part.

Moses' Rejection of the Shepherd's Hymns (I)

Moses saw a shepherd along the road,
saying O' God you are my chosen Lord.
Where are you so I render to you my work;
comb your hair and sew your clothes.
I will wash you body and kill your lice,
bring you warm milk with something nice.
I will kiss your hands and rub your feet
before bed time you'll find your bed neat.
For you I will sacrifice all my goats
I will chant heeha from my throat
rubbish and rage are these words.
Moses asked, who are these words for?
The shepherd said these special words,
are for the creator of the two worlds.
Moses said are you an authority or a cardinal?
or before learning the faith, became an infidel.
What manners what rage are these words;
stuff cotton in your mouth and behold.
Your septic thoughts will infect the world;
your mouth discharges incoherent words.
Shirts and socks are for our bodies and feet;
our Lord for these things has no needs.
If you are not quiet and shut your mouth,
mankind will be punished from your thoughts.
When there is no fire, what is this smoke?
If the spirit is blackened, why reject the soul?
If you know the Lord is the ultimate judge,
why in insolence you babble so much.
Friendship to ignorance is having foes;
the gracious Lord has needs not your toys.
Who are you talking to your uncle or aunt?
Your life and body are at mercy of His hand.
The milk is for an infant who needs to grow,
hat keeps the head warm in cold and snow.
If the Lord for his creatures has some words,
you hear it from me, assume it is from the Lord.
He who claimed I didn't visit him while he was ill,
he was well with visitors, but I wasn't well.
The one who hears none and sees none,
to the audience of the Lord he will not come.
To speak and not follow the rules of the Lord,
will blacken your card, suppresses your soul.
If you call a man Fathima for his name,

though men and women are the same,
he will attempt to kill you out of his rage;
though he may be kind and gentle by his traits.
It is an honor for a woman to have this name;
but for a man brings raging shame.
He is fit to say "not born nor will bear,"
since he made those who were born and will bear.
The one in substance is the one born;
the one who bears has escaped this world.
The one in existence is corrupt with grace;
he is fresh in need of the guidance of the great.

The Lord Talks to Moses Regarding the Shepherd (II)

Moses heard a voice from above,
saying you alienated our servant in love.
You were assigned to make my people join,
not to hurt their feelings on your own.
Division is loathed by every man
try to avoid this work if you can.
I made diverse faiths with different psalms;
I bestowed many melodies in their hymns.
A blasphemy to one, to another a faith;
sugar to one , to another poisonous taste.
Chastity and immodesty are made for all;
sluggish and witty are found in all.
I did not make these for profits and gains,
I gave them love , hearts and brains.
For gentle Hindus a way fitting their land;
Parsis pray holding barsam in his hands.
No gain comes to me from rosary and pray;
but they gain by following their ways.
I look not at their religious choice;
I look for purity in their souls.
I seek their hearts for the honesty;
not to mannerism nor dignity.
The essence is heart covered with talks;
talk is the music but the lyrics are the hearts.
We stayed too long for ceremonies and talks;
I want the flames that burns the hearts.
The fire of love starts from the hearts;
its flame will burn the remaining talks.
Followers of Moses with their blessed way;
followers of love have the burning flames.
Each breath of the lover will burn their lives;

the slaves in ruins, no earnings nor costs.
If he made an error call it no wrong;
bathe him not when covered in blood.
Beyond things is the worth of his blood;
this wrong is favored over the other right.
No need is for the compass when at the pole;
the diver in deep has no need for snow.
From those who tear do not expect to mend;
from those in love do not ask to lead.
From religions the way of love is apart;
lovers race and religion is God.
The gem is not concern with its essay;
love from the sea of sorrow is away.

Revelations to Moses in Forgiving the Shepherd (III)

Then came a message from the Lord;
revealed to Moses in secret words.
Then to Moses came many thoughts;
his thoughts and insight were mixed in one.
He went to trance in trance of trance;
from naught he returned to existence.
If further on this matter I should talk,
 a warning I see coming from afar.
If I indulge more will shatter the brain;
if I write further will break the pen.
As Moses heard these messages from God,
ran after the shepherd in the wild.
The one in dilemma acts in peculiar ways;
random manners comes to his pace.
One step in certain sure as a rook;
another, a hesitant elephant crossing a brook.
At time a ship riding majestically on waves;
at times, as Jonah in belly of the whale.
At times carved clearly on tablets of clay;
at times shamefully hiding in a stack of hay.
Moses found the shepherd at last;
said: be glad, I have good news for fact.
There is no unaccepted way to pray;
whatever you wish you may say.
Your wrong is a faith, the light of the souls;
your certainty brings a promise to the world
free from the sermons of religious world,
without reservation you may say your words.
The shepherd told Moses these I passed;

in my own blood I am sitting at last.
Through thousand years I have gone;
on many roads and placed I was bound.
You came and gave my horse the final lash;
then from the earth and heavens it passed.
My sins were the righteous in my way;
I salute your endeavor in your way.
The way I feel is beyond words,
for my feeling is beyond this world.
The refection in the mirror in your view;
is not from the mirror, but it is from you.
(Rumi, II, 1720)

In the first part of the story, Moses tells a shepherd that he prays incorrectly. Moses imagines that the Lord will not appreciate the shepherds offerings. However, what Moses does not understand is that to the shepherd, the things he offers are luxurious and worthy.

In the second part of the story, the Lord points out that He has created many religions and faiths on purpose, and that the shepherd's prayer is not less significant than any of Moses' prayers.

In the third part, Moses returns to the shepherd and apologizes to him. The shepherd is grateful but does not need the apology since he has already attained incarnation and felt the presence of the Lord.

The following odes are representative of the many odes written by prominent Sufi masters.

Unknown

I known not who I am, tell my friends what to do;
for I am not a Moslem, not a Christian, nor a Jew.
Not of east nor of west, not of hills nor of shores
not of earth nor of turning planets in the orb.
Not of soils nor of waters, not of wind nor of fire;
not of throne, nor of commons, not of those with ire.
Not a Bulgar, nor a Chinese, not a Hindu with a mole
not an Arab, nor a Persian, not a Turk with a sword.
Not of religion nor of faith, nor of heavens with stars;
not of Adam with his Eve, nor of Eden with its trees.
Not of a place in a place, not of a trail with a trace.
The life I have is of different kind, which is none.
The worlds of two, I see one, for that two, is really one;
now I seek, as I say, as I know as I sing only one.
This start is its end; this is the surface and its depth;
Him and me, is all I know other ways, I know not.
I am in trance of my life, the world of two, I forgot,
the work of thugs is all I know, other work I know not.
If I breath without him, sorrow will befall on me,
sadness with its dark clouds fills the hour of my time.
With a Friend if I have but a moment of my time,
the worlds will come beneath my feet, if I raise just a hand.
I am a bird, but the kind that can fly in its egg.
I have life, I have love, with the body made of clay.
Help me Shams, in this world, I am in trance,
as you know, in this life, I am a thug, in a dance.
(Rumi, Book of Shams)

Rumi expresses his difference from the rest of the world and asks Shams, his mentor, to help him define himself in a seemingly unfamiliar world.

The Way of Love
O' Bartender fill my glass with red wine;
I'm in trouble with this love of mine.
The fragrance of the morning breeze will undo,
the Beloved's wavy tress that broke my heart.
Cannot enjoy my stay in this house of love,
since each minute the caller may terminate my time.
If the Pier orders wash in sins the holy books,
worry not the Pier is aware of the ways of other houses.
In a dark night in a turbulent sea with giant waves,
unaware are those asleep in the safety of their homes.
Disgrace was brought to my name by my selfish work,
how long hidden will it be the secret we waited for.
Hafez absent do not be if His audience you should seek
trivial becomes everything if the Beloved I could meet.
(Hafez, Ode #1)

Hafez discusses the difficult path of Sufism. He speaks of the obstacles and burdens the Sufi must overcome. However, in the end, when a Sufi encounters the Lord, all struggles will appear trivial.

Advice of the Magian Boy

Went to the tavern, tired and dozed,
in wine my rosary and cloak were soaked.
Contrite Magian boy sold the wine;
told me: beware, you ordinary clown.
Before entering this tavern, you must bathe,
to keep this ancient place free of stains.
How long did you covet kisses from nymphs,
that stains the soul with liquid gems?
Go with purity through the house of the Piers,
with no youth's protocols and degrading deeds.
Pure and clean rise from the temporal wells,
gain no pleasures from water of smells.
I asked O' Great: would it be wrong,
to stain the Spring flowers with wine?
The acquaintance of the Lover's Lane,
though submerged in sea, are not stained.
Said, Hafez don't offer hints and slanders to friends;
pity, by harsh words His kindness is stained.
(Hafez, Divan, Ode #419)

In this ode Hafez encounters a boy from the Magian priest class. The boy gives him advice as to what to do and expect. When Hafez asserts that Sufi cannot be "stained," no matter how far into the depths they tread, the Magian boy warns him not to become too proud.

Reflection of Your Face

As the mirror of challis smilingly reflected your image
for their fantasies the philosopher paid homage.
As the beauty of your lineament appeared once in the
wine,
so many silhouettes came to the mirror of the mind.
Many reflections in the wine and the diverse faces,
are from the glow of the face of the Giver of challis.
The pride of Love stole the intimates' tongue
then why do others talk of the sorrows secret so long?
I left the Mosque for the Temple not by accident,
this had been my predestined reward.
Unable to escape the tether of time
what is my role in the circle of thine.
You saved me from the well by the lock of your tress,
pity, I was trapped by beguile and ruse.
You see me ended here the temple with lepers,
now my work is Beloved's face and the lips of challis.
Jubilantly go dancing under the sword of remorse
lucky and blessed is the one who is in pieces.
Each moment he has a new bait for my aching heart,
surprise, the beggar qualified for the prize.
The Sufi are watchful, eager contenders,
only Hafez became the one branded.
(Hafez, Ode #107)

Hafez discusses the idea of seeing the reflection of the Lord through our hearts. Although different people may see different reflections, the Lord remains the same.

Hafez also acknowledges the problems he has had following the Sufi way. He explains that he feels trapped by time and other worldly things and wanted to be reunited with the Lord.

Pretentious

For those who with their eyes turn soil to alchemy,
would it be possible to take a glimpse at me.
Hiding my pain is better than seeing a pretentious heal-
er,
I may be cured from the medicine of unseen treasures.
Since the beloved does not remove her veil,
why do they tell these fantasy tales?
Since our reward is not for our deity or deceit,
it is better to perform only prudent deeds.
To the tools of love do not be blind,
for the sellers deal only with trusted friends.
Salute the covered sins, drink the wine,
much seditious work is done in the name of the Divine.
I am afraid the shirt that carries David's scent,
the bold brothers will make a holy cloak from it.
Much sedition is done behind the veil;
if the curtains are removed, what will they tell?
Do not be amazed if rocks cry from these tales;
the chosen have heart pleasing stories to tell.
Pass by the crowd of the winery road,
ask them to pray for your soul.
Hidden from the jealous, tell me that our denial,
is His Benevolence's hidden approval.
O' Hafez His audience can not last forever,
the Lord shows little kindness to the pauper.
(Hafez, Divan, Ode# 193)

Hafez describes those who could help him reach perfection and those whose "eyes turn soil to alchemy" seeking the tools that can lead him to the Lord. He enlists the help of the crowd at the winery who, in Islamic tradition, are people from the lowest class to pray for his soul.

Trance in the Wine

The mirror of purity is the cup, O Sufi;
look for the trance through its color of ruby.
Ask the drunk thugs the secrecy of the veil;
to reach it through the pious ways will fail.
The bird of the mystic will not land
pick up the trap, nothing comes to your hand.
Drink only a cup and then leave the dance
do not be eager to last long in his audience.
Picked no flowers and your youth is passed;
do not disgrace yourself now with foolish acts.
With the love at hand, endeavor your best;
the Garden of Eden not even to Adam did last.
To your threshold we have done much service;
O Lord with mercy look toward your slaves.
Morning breeze, Hafez is a fool for some wine;
from slaves send slavery to the Sheik of Wine.
(Hafez, Ode #6)

Hafez states that one can gain insight by listening to "drunk thugs," a term used in Sufi writings to refer to "unpolished people." As it is the case in other religions, Sufi masters did not put much faith in other religious leaders and their understanding of the "Truth." Hafez also notes that the highest concepts are not easily understood.

His Appearance

Each moment in different shapes the idol in disguise
appears,
breaks our hearts and disappears.
Each moment with different garments the friend
appears,
at times young, and at times old.
At times sinks deep to the heart of the earth for essence,
seeking the truth.
At times comes as a proud single piece of clay,
becomes a fetus.
What is abolition, migrations of the souls to the Lord,
the heart breaking beauty.
Became a sword in the hands of the conqueror,
the killer of time.
Roamed the land and the sea for while,
for pleasure.
Became Jesus to the revolving world,
rosary in his hand.
Became Noah, who with prayer flooded the world,
boarded the Ark,
Became a friend and emerged from the heart of a tree,.
the reddish of the flowers.
Became Joseph, who from Egypt sent the shirt,
enlightened the world.
From the eyes of Jacob glowed as lights,
became visible.
By truth, it was him who was doing the work of a shepherd,
with the miraculous hands.
Once became a wooden stick to the traits of a serpent,
the sea of foams.
Became pious and asked the people to join the way,
for their own good.
Became a camel appeared in the mountains,
suddenly visible.
The brain that grew to be learned, wise and complete,
suddenly old;
became happily drunk on the mountain top,
better than young.
Became Job who patiently waited in the city of Kerman,
he was pain and cure;
from the depth of the heart cried behold,
his eye were life.
Became Jonas in the belly of a fish in the sea,
to be cleansed.
Became Moses who demanded to see,

46

sought Mount Sinai.
Became Jesus who from the cradle gave the testimony.
to the Holy Spirit;
from his miracles the trees bore fruits,
the spirits flew;
cut the moon in half, by the order of his figure,
the way of beloved;
became the full moon and appeared again,
departure of the souls;
praised by the Angels, the leader of the army of souls.
the holy spirit.
Shaped a piece of wood and attached strings,
the instrument of the world.
Hundreds moans and cries came from each string,
became loud.
By God, it was he who comes and goes,
as you see in each century.
Finally appeared in the fashions of an Arab,
owned the world.
By God, it was he who was saying I am the truth,
in the voice of the Lord.
It was not Mansour who was on the gallows.
unaware of thoughts.
Even now he is not invisible, look and try to see,
with the inner eyes.
It is him that all these talks are about,
became visible to the eyes.
Rumi never had nor ever will utter blasphemy;
do not disbelieve in him.
Tabriz was him and he, the Sun of essence,
in the flower garden of lights.
It was him who appeared in ebullitions of the secrets,
a mark in love.
(Rumi, Book of Shams)

Rumi alludes to the omnipresence of the Lord that exists in every tradition and culture the world has known.

Section II:
Affliction of the Roses

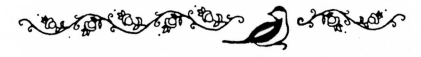

This section consists of two parts: The *Words of Ecstasy* and *The Martyrs*. The *Words of Ecstasy* lead to the eventual executions of the *Martyrs*.

The Words of Ecstasy

I am the singer of the ode of ecstasy,
the words are true, for its proof is thee
(Attar, Divan, Ode #793)

Expressing the thoughts of eternity using our vocabulary is not an easy task. In addition to describing the eternal world, problems Sufi struggled with in their writings were the feeling of the "union" and the feeling of reaching eternity. Since Sufi faith is also called the "path of love," Sufi poetry and prose at times resembles a conversations between two lovers or appears as a lonely lover's lament. To express their feelings the Sufi use words such as "wine," "cup," "jug" which are are meant to be taken as metaphors.

Poetic thoughts can help one imagine places such as eternity and the dwelling of the Lord, as well as the travels of the souls from the world of eternity to the land of time. The soul is saddened when it departs from the world of light, and upon reaching its destination, the newborn cries, expressing the feeling of the soul. Hence, Rumi starts his *Book of the Reed* with "Harken, harken to this reed forlorn, breathing ever since was torn."

Habits may be controlled by Sufi teachings and exercises. These teachings consist of studying religious and Sufi books as well as etiquette, meditations, and leading an ascetic life. These actions enable the Sufi to reach his extraordinary perceptions to receive messages from beyond. Learning and attaining the qualities of a Sufi is commonly compared to the journey of a novice on unfamiliar roads and through dangerous mountains and valleys. All exercises will lead the student to a Sufi's final destination: the exalting feeling of attaining incarnation, the "hulul," when the Sufi unites with the Lord.

We find various views regarding the meaning of *shat'h (The Words of Ecstasy)*. For example, some claim that *shat'h* has religious connotations. This leads to the paradoxical use of the *Shat'hiat* which gives the Sufi certain liberties when speaking these words without being blamed for blasphemy. Others believe that *shat'h* is a secret language invented by the Sufi in order to be able to communicate in secret.

It cannot be denied that *The Words of Ecstacy* present views that are opposed to basic Islamic teachings. *Shat'hiat* writings have caused problems and, at times, lead to the execution of Sufi masters. An example of bold *Shat'hiat* writings by Omar Khayyam reads:

> The Koran that is called the Lord's verses,
> is read from time to times but not always,
> but there is a verse about the challis
> for which it is called upon always.

Khayyam suggests that Muslims refer to some parts of the Koran more often than to others.

In *Heiloge Nameh* (The Letter of the Reason of Life), Attar describes the person who brings the wine as the cupbearer "Soughi" which is considered a sacrilege according to the Islamic faith:

> As the cupbearer handed me a cup,
> on my own I opened the bottle of wine.
> The silhouette of the cupbearer, I see,
> but to describe it is beyond me.
> The cupbearer is always in my life,
> helps me to see the secrets of love.
> Look at the cupbearer inside of me;
> tells me the tales of the wine in winery.
> From the wine that is hard to bear,
> except for Mansour none can bear.
> If in doubts, look at the turning heaven,
> the cupbearer came to us to remain.
> Her scent was discovered by the stars;
> the reason they revolve around us.
> *(Attar, HN, 311, 81)*

These *Shath'iat* along with the Sufi *Sam'a* (the Sufi gathering) could be misused by a novice who lacks the required understanding of Sufi thoughts. In fact, some Sufi orders gradually became corrupt because they tolerated excessive drinking and dancing and other unwarranted behaviors.

Abu al Farj, a Sufi opponent, in *Teblis al Eblis* regarding the Sam'a dancing and happiness writes, "Beware that singing in their gathering has two reasons: first, the heart will be restrained from thinking of the greatness of the Lord and the desire of serving Him, and secondly, man will desire momentary pleasures, especially sexual pleasures. And, since sexual pleasures vary from women to women, this desire will not be satisfied except by committing sins. Thus, hearing these songs will encourage man to comit adultery because songs are the pleasure of the soul and adultery is the highest pleasure of the body...."

Aside from the seductive character of Sufi love poems, the problem of the renegade elements appeared as the foremost problem. To correct the problem, Ghashiri (circa 1222) wrote his *Resalet* to reinstate Sufi principles for guiding the followers. *The Words of Ecstasy,* however, may not necessarily be anti-religious. Consider, for example, the following poem:

Life I am, but the kind you do not see;
as the moon, in no one place I be.
I glow to the stars and the moon;
I am the sun in the sky of certainty.
I am the Giaour that gave birth to belief,
but secure and safe I am in my blasphemy.
I am the spell that entered Merriem,
the spirit that made Jesus walk on the sea,
the part that gave birth to the whole and,
the part that is whole life and matter is me,
belonging to the other world but here I am;
I know that there is no one else but me.
In essence between this and that I am;
I was praised by Mansour and Shebli.
Wrapped between the veils of kindness and life,
I will remain for a thousand centuries.
If I cover my eyes shut,
the silhouette of the friend I will still see.
Silence will come to me if Shams orders;
then, the tongue of the silence I shall be.
(Rumi, Book of Shams)

Rumi describes the joyous feeling of incarnation, or oneness with the Lord. He also mentions the praise he has received and his belief that he is the only Sufi to reach the state of incarnation.

To explain meaning and purpose of using the *shat'hiat,* we can turn to Mahmud Shabestari, a Sufi of the fourteen century. His most famous work is *Golshanraz* (The Secrets of the Flower Garden) which consists of one thousand verses and provides the answers to seventeen questions that regard the meaning of Amir Sid Husain Harvi Husaini's writings. I have translated a small portion of his writing to illuminate the subject.

Question:
What is meant by "the candle, witness and wine?"
What does it mean to join "the winery crowd?"

Answer:
The wine, witness, candle stand for their intent;
since each from His greatness is to reflect.
From the art of Sufi are born these three;
the witness is visible, try to see.
Wine from the cup, the candle for light;
the glow of the witness is the soul's light.
The witness excited Moses' heart,
his candle the tree, the wine firing hot.
The captives' light are wine, candle, and cup;
the witness remains as those heavenly songs.

The candle, the witness, the wine are with us;
but beware of the witness' final act.
Only at times drink the worthless wine,
if you desire to be free for a while.
Drink the wine that frees yourself from you;
that takes to the sea the essence of dew.
Drink the wine of the cup bearing His face;
the vision-giving cup from the rummy place.
Seek the wine not of the challis nor of jars;
seek the one the cupbearer gets from the bars.
Drink the wine from the remaining means,
O' Lord, O' thirst quencher the cup bearer is His.
The wine, cleanser of the worldly muck,
which cleanses as you become drunk.
Drink the wine and free yourself from the cold;
better to be drunk than aware and bold.
Whoever is distant from the threshold of Truth,
better than light is to cover his gloom.
Even from the dark help came to man,
but the light had eternally cursed Satan.
If the mirror is covered totally by sooth,
for seeing an image, will serve no use.
The glow of his reflection in the wine,
creates bubbles of various size.
Life and form are in globule shape;
the globules making the cupola for Saints.
From him the brain is baffled in trance;
it totally has enslaved the essence.
The world is his fermenting, boiling from top;
the heart of each speckle is his measuring cup.
The Angels, thoughts, lives are in trance;
the air, the earth the skies are in trance.
The stars are orbiting to find his trace;
the air is searching for the scent of His place.
The Angels drank from the cup, straight;
a small amount was spilled on earth.
From the spill the nature came to joy;
at times in fire, or in water, cold.
From his reflection the ill became well;
from his glow the spirit became soul.
From the scent of the spill that came down,
the man was raised and flew to the skies.
From Him the creatures of the world are lost;
their belonging and lives they forgot.
From the fragrance, one became wise;
from its colors, one began to write.
One became honest by half of a gulp;
another fell in love by drinking a cup.

One in recluse, a hermit a punk;
from the cup, the wine, the drunk.
From this all are amazed, surprised;
a thug with a great heart full of pride.
He has the essence of existence inside,
free of confessions, shames and denials.
Free from the dry piety and babble talk;
holding to the Peir of the winery crowd.
(Shabestari, Golshan Raz, 804)

Explaining *The Words of Ecstacy* Shabestari writes:

The Tress
The tale of the tress of the mistress is long;
we reach the unknown, I can be wrong .
Ask me not of the tale of the wavy tress;
rattle not the cage of the crazy in chains.
I spoke of her silhouette last night;
the lock of her tress told me to quit.
(Shabestari, Golshan Raz, 763)

Question:
What is meant by "pointing to eyes and marks of the
face?"
What does the learned seek in trance
from the face, the tress, and the lips?

Answer:
Whatever is clearly seen in this world,
is only the reflection of the other world.
The world as the eyes, the tress, the mole;
each is pleasant in the spot of its own.
The beauty, the glory come in his show ,
for metaphor we use the words we know.
We see, we feel, we use the words we heard,
the object is to try to explain the way we felt.
The traits of the Lord is harsh and kind;
for those the terms of face, the tress are fine.
No limits nor end are in the eternal world;
how can this be expressed with our words?
Thus these selective words used for taste,
their intent cannot be easily explained.
(Shabestari, Golshan Raz, 717)

See what is apparent from the witness' eyes
be careful, use the proper tools with protocols.
From the eyes came the malice and trance;

from the lips came the eyes of existence.
From the eyes the hearts have fallen in trance;
the ruby lips covered the lives with curtains.
The hearts are broken by the beauty of the eyes,
the remedy for the sick came from the mouth.
Though the world cannot understand the eyes,
the ruby lips keep sending kindness to us.
(Shabestari, Golshan Raz, 744)

The Martyrs

I am a ball in the field of time of the months and years
in the polo of the fate, I am hit to roll from here to there
(Abdul Raham Jami)

Less than a century after the victorious Islamic army established the Holy Koran in the land of the followers of the Holy Avesta, we find scattered appearances of the early Sufi in the Islamic empire. Sufism sprang up everywhere, in the flourishing city of Baghdad, as well as in the distant provinces. We know of Ebrahiem Adham (d. circa 782) in Balkh, one of the eastern cities in the province of Khorasan and of Abu Hashem (d. circa 782), who was the first person in Basrah to be called a Sufi. The first Sufi sheikh of the Baghdad order was Abu Eshaq Balkhi (d. circa 872). Abul Faiez Zol Funun (d. circa 866) was the first Sufi in Egypt to be considered a heretic.

The early Sufi carried out the Muslim way of worshipping (cleaning themselves, praying and fasting) in an extreme way. Their leaders were well educated in the Holy Koran, the Hadith and the Islamic laws. They related all their thoughts to the Holy Koran and described themselves as "... [those] whose soul is free from resentment and [whose] heart is full of the thoughts of the Lord.... *(T.O.)*" Early Sufism was considered a separate Islamic religion posing a potential threat to the empire.

Ask not to lead from the one in trance,
ask not to mend from the one who tears.
The nation of Love is apart from faiths;
the Lord is their religion and their race.
The gem is not worried from its assay;
love in not grieved by the mournful sea.
(Rumi, II, 1769-1771)

Three renown Sufi, Nuri, Hallaj and Ain al Ghozzat were accused of blasphemy and heresy and were executed. We will briefly look at the sagas of Nuri and Hallaj in writings of other Sufi. Nuri and Hallaj are considered to belong to the "Tarigheh Sek'r" (a school of the extreme right) whereas most other Sufi are considered to belong to a moderate school, "Tarigheh Sah'v" (Sober).

Alboul Hassan Nuri (d. 907), "who was attracted to the oneness, who was swept away by the glory, the source of light, the center of the secrets, who donated himself for longing, the elegant Aboul Hassan Nuri" was a brave man with an impressive nature, who did not avoid danger to shield his brethren. Nuri declared that "...to be a Sufi is neither a tradition nor a science; it is inborn since if it were a tradition, it could be forced on people, and if it were a science, it could be learned. It is from the Lord, and thus its manifestation is neither scientific nor traditional..." *(T.O.* 543*)*. Baba Taher Hamedani, known as Orian (Naked), a Sufi of the eleventh century, expresses Nuri's idea:

> This love came to me as I was born
> not from the teaching, nor my forlorn
> happy for my lament, not in vain,
> the day my love come to cure my pain.
> *(Baba Taher Orian)*

Nuri was quoted to have said: "...(human) reasoning is weak and (because of its weakness) can only understand weak postulates...," "There was a frail old man who endured (the punishment of many) lashes with patience and then he was taken to jail. I asked him, How could you, in your weak condition, bear such (severe) punishment? He replied, With desire (from the soul) you can bear the mishap but you cannot do the same with with the body alone. Then, I asked, What is patience to you? He replied that what brings you into danger as well as what brings you out of it."

"Sufi are those whose hearts are free of resentment and whose thoughts are free from malice of selfishness and (unwanted) desires. They can stand in front of the queues facing the Truth, and they desire none but Him; they do not possess anything nor are they possessed. To be a Sufi means to be free-spirited, having chivalry in one's heart and be generous but without pride."

"It is said that one day Nuri went to the mosque where Shebli was giving a sermon. As Nuri entered, he said greetings to 'the First' and Shebli replied by saying Greetings to 'the Prince of the Hearts.' Nuri said that the Lord does not like the learned who teaches but does not follow his own teaching. Shebi paused and thought of his own deeds, then stepped down from the podium, left and stayed in his house for months until his followers asked him to return to his work of giving sermons. Nuri was informed of (Shebli's return) and came to Shebli's assembly and told Shebli that for covering the truth, they returned you to the work of giving sermons, but for giving advice, they chased me with stones toward the garbage dump."

"Oh God will you torture those committed to hell, those with commitments of the science and the perseverance of the ancient times? Undoubtedly hell will be filled with them. Can you fill hell and its layers with me and set the others free in Paradise *(T.O.)*?"

Nuri recalls: "I saw a light of unseen and as I stared at it I became that light..." Let us compare Nuri's saying with the Koran, Sura Al Nur Verses (24.34). "God is the Light [the giver of the Light] of heaven and earth and his light resembles a niche with a light in it and that light is encased in a bulb as a glowing star from the blessed olive tree. Although [the Light] is neither from the East nor the West, it lightens the East and the West and, without being a fire, it gives light to the world and its glow will enlighten the guiding lights and the Lord guides the chosen to be guided, and the Lord knows all." Although the Holy Koran is concerned with guiding believers, and Nuri is claiming to be that (guiding) light, the effect is similar.

Nuri clearly was a man of devotion. Not only was he devoted to the Lord but also to the people of the Lord. However, despite his noble intentions, Nuri and his followers were accused of being Zoroastrians and vegetarians were branded as Zandagheh by Ghulam Khalil (888), a strict Muslim who did not tolerate any deviations from the exact words of the prophet Mohammad. Ghulam tried Nuri and his followers. Here is an excerpt of Hajviri's description of the trial:

"...and the truth in giving is that one should keep what truly belongs to the master and should give his portion also to his master and should bear the discomfort for pleasing his master...It is said that when Gholam Khalil showed his animosity to this group and brought them forth for many accusations and arrested Nuri, Ragham and Abu Hamzeh and took all three to the capitol building. Ghulam sent a message to the khalief claiming that this group is of Zandagheh faith and if the khalief orders their execution the nucleus of Zandagheh will be destroyed since these are the leaders. The khalief ordered their execution and the executioner came and he tied their hands and prepared them for the execution. As the execution was prepared, Nuri stood up and walked towards the cutting stole, convinced and happy to such an extend that the audience was amazed. The executioner said [to Nuri], 'Oh gentle person, this sword is not so precious to come forth for so eagerly as you have done, besides it is not your turn yet.' Nuri replied: 'This selflessness is my way and [to me] it is the highest quality of life and I wish to spare these few breaths of life for my friends and one breath of life is better for me than a thousand from the other world since this is the world of giving and the other is the world of intimacy and intimacy is gained by serving.' This conversation was relayed to the khalief who was impressed by [Nuri's] kind character and ability to phrase thoughts so eloquently that he sent a messenger to cancel the execution.

The judge Abbas ebin Ali took the convicts to his house and tested them for their knowledge of the laws and the principles of the religion. Whatever he asked they answered [correctly].... Then Nuri said to the judge: 'You have asked all the questions but you did not ask who the Lord's men are that revolt against friends and have taken His oath in words and deeds and lean on the Lord....' The judge was impressed by Nuri's eloquence and the depth of the wording and the sincerity of his feelings. He wrote to the khalief stating that if these [convicts] were the atheists, he would testify and proclaim that there was no pious person on this earth. The khalief called for them to be brought before him and [upon their arrival] asked them to make a wish. They replied, 'We wish that you to forget us and not to make us neither your confidants nor banned. Your distance to us is your acceptance and your acceptance is distance.' This made the kahlief weep and with kindness he allowed them to return (K. M. 236)."

Khalief Al Muwafegh, impressed with Nuri's thoughts and knowledge, gave Nuri complete freedom of speech. Nuri enjoyed this freedom for a while but later, during the reign of Al Mu'tadid, turmoil and the uprising within the empire changed the political atmosphere. The new Khalief Al Mu'tadid became weary of the spread of Zandagheh and Nuri was brought to trial again. This time he was not as fortunate as before, and his Nuri's execution was ordered.

Attar describes Husain Ibn Mansour al-Hallaj as "[t]he one who was killed for the Lord, following the Lord's way, the lion of the meadow of discovery, the ripper [of the curtain of the secrets], righteous and brave, submerged in the turbulent sea: Housain Mansour Hallaj, God bless, his work was wonders of the times. Burning with love till his death...intoxicated by the trance of the time, he was a sincere and true lover, radiant with infinite energy, ascetic yet generous... His many biographies contain difficult words concerning the secret of Truth and the ultimate kindness. He was a good speaker unlike others, with a keen vision unlike others. Most of the great [the Sufi masters] disagreed with him except for a few such as Abdalah Khalief, Shebli and Abol Ghasem Ghoshari(*T. O.* 666)."

Hallaj was born in what is today the city of Tur in southwestern Iran. His father was a converted Moslem and his grandfather a orthodox Zoroastrian. Hallaj soon became one of the Nuri's disciples. Ebn Nadiem recorded that Mansour ebn Hallaj wrote forty six books, among them *Ketab Elm al Bagha* (The Book of the Knowledge of Eternity) and *Ketab al Yaghien* (The Book of Certainty). Neither Hallaj's works nor other books produced by other Sufi writers of this period have survived.

Hallaj was well versed in the Holy Koran and the Hadith, but he stayed defiant towards the establishment and believed that the true way of worshipping came from within. He strongly believed in incarnation (hulul). Hallaj suggested that a replica of Mecca be built in Baghdad where he was residing at the time. Moslems, wishing to travel to Mecca, should come to this replica instead of going all the way to Mecca. Hallaj proposed to donate the traveling expenses the wayfarers would save to orphanages.

Attar writes that when Hallaj was united with the Truth he thought he had become the Truth instead of realizing that he was only a small part of the Truth. Sufi philosophy states that when a dervish joins the Truth, it resembles a droplet that joins the infinite sea. The droplet can not claim to be the eternal sea. When a person is united with the Truth, the religious rites and blasphemy become the same. After Hallaj's death, three groups of Sufi--one in Khorasan, one in Fars and the other in Iraq--claimed to be the followers of Hallaj. Today, the Fariyeh followers see themselves as Hallaj's followers.

Shebli remembered Housain (Hallaj). "The first day I went to see Housain, he was talking [about some subjects] which I did not understand, because understanding it was not permissible. But what I remembered was that he said, 'O Lord in each Hagh (title) there is a truth, and in each person a path, and in each promise a pledge,' and then he said, 'O Shebli, the secret exists but hidden in the language of this tribe, and its meaning is with them.' Shebli further relates that Hallaj continued explaining, 'The Truth created the hearts and in them bestowed is his secret. Man was [then] created and a curtain was placed between the heart and the secret. Knowledge was placed in desire and Truth is [hidden] in secret. No breath will be taken without the order of the Oneness [the Lord] and the reason of knowledge is within the desires for the world of the Lord... (*Rozbehan Baghli, Sharh Shathiat* 380, 381).'"

Hallaj was brought to trial several times. Each time the trial ended with minor or no convictions. In one trial he was placed under house arrest and lived in the Caliph's court-at times in chains, other times comfortably. However, the last trial was overseen by Chancellor Hamied, one of Hallaj's advisors, who were quick to accuse Hallaj of claiming divine lordship and preaching incarnation as well as using names for the Lord not found in the Koran such as the "God of the Gods." Although not all present agreed with Hallaj's conviction, Hamied nevertheless made sure that any opposition was removed or silenced. The execution was carried out in 922.

Hallaj removed the veil from the secret in such a way that commoners called him "infidel" and the Sufi masters called him "insane." The moderate Sufi believe that Sufi should obey religious rites and never give away secrets to outsiders. Hafez writes:

The one that gallows became holy from touch
his guilt was revealing the secret of the Truth
(Hafez, Divan)

Attar writes about Hallaj:

As toward the gallows Hallaj walked,
nothing but "the truth" came to his mouth.
From the cuts he began to bleed;
pity, they did not understand his deeds.
From loosing blood, he became pale,
for the blood gives the color to the face.
Swiftly he rubbed his blood to his face,
the face of the sun, the light of our ways.
Said, the blood in vane is, the color to the face,
thus with my own blood I colored my face.
Now I will appear to none as pale,
for this red will be the color of my face.
Since to whoever I appear pale,
they may think that I was afraid.
But since of nothing I am afraid,
I have no pale color in my face.
The one by the gallows with such a face,
his deeds are of the lion with grace
as this world is a blessed ring.
Why should I be afraid of what I sing?
The one who sleeps and eats, always
with the seven-headed dragon for days,
many a time he had fallen to falls.
The fall to gallows is the smallest fall.
(Attar, M.T, 2287)

Attar describes Hallaj as the sun, bringing light, the way of the Sufis to all his
followers. A true Sufi, Hallaj faced his death without fear.

Sufi have questioned Hallaj's unjust punishment and have related his experiences to the story of "the tree that caught fire upon realizing the greatness of the Lord."
The tree exclaimed "I am the Truth." Why could Hallaj not claim to be the Truth? I provide Shabestari's answer to the question of "I am the Truth":

Question
What point signifies that "I am the Truth?"
Why do you call it babble, the secret of absolute?

Answer
"I am the Truth" is the discovery of the absolute;
none but the "truth" can claim this to be true.
The world, the speckles, as Mansour:
whether, sober or insane you may assume.

With rosary uttering their psalms;
convinced with the theme of their thoughts.
If you wish to reach this goal with ease;
stop saying I came from material and things.
as you prepare and work as Mansour,
"I am the Truth" also will be coming from you.
Remove the barriers of thoughts from your ears,
so you can hear the call of success.
The call of Truth is coming to you always;
why are you donated to the judgement day?
Go by the veil of the truth and become free
or you will hear the call of truth from a tree.
It is fitting for a tree to claim this truth;
but not fitting for the brave Mansour.
The one with no doubts in his heart,
knows for certain there is only one.
This oneness is fitting for the truth,
but is hidden from the senses in you..
The Holy Saint of truth is not in two;
the Saint knows "no me," no us," "no you."
(Shabestary Golshanraz, 436)

Shabestari speaks of Hallaj's claims of being the Truth. He speaks of the absurdity of a tree claiming to be "the Truth" and explains that Hallaj was executed for making a similarily ridiculous claim.

Section III:
The Seeds of the Flowers

This section explains Sufi training, in Sufi writings referred to as *the path.* Here is an description by Attar from the *Mantgh al tayre:*

> There are seven valleys along our road,
> once one is passed, it becomes a threshold.
> From there no one returned to this world,
> to tell the conditions of the road
> since no one returned from this road,
> how can we describe it, behold.
> The valley of desire on this road comes first,
> second the valley of love comes next.
> The valley of knowledge is the third on the road.
> The valley of independence is the fourth abode.
> The sacred valley of oneness comes fifth.
> The feared valley of bewilderment is sixth.
> Seventh is poverty, the valley of naught.
> Then no more valleys comes to your sight.
> (Attar, M. T., 3225)

In the past, Sufi training consisted of two distinct elements: studying and inner training of feelings and mind. The learned parts are called "paths" and the part pertaining to feelings are called "trances." Many books have been written on these two parts of Sufi training. Abul Haasan al Hajviri Ghaznavi (d. circa 1077), in *Kashf al Mahjoob* (Discovery of the Grace) writes about the past Islamic saints, the Sufi peir as well as the Sufi ways. Aboul Ghasem Ghariri (d. circa 1075) in his *Resalat* writes about the stages one must go through in order to become a Sufi. *Resalat* covers stages as well as the required behavior for aspiring Sufis. The first section of *Nafhat al Rooh va Tohfat al Fotooh* (The Wind of the Soul and the Prize of Reaching), a work of the latter-day Sufi Moayed al Din Jondi (d. circa 1312), covers religious sciences and philosophy and the second section covers the work of the followers of the path.

The descriptions of the stages and trances varies from one Sufi order to another. For example, grades and levels of stages and trances overlap each other. For the purpose of this book, I have chosen only the most common grades and levels developed by Abu Nasr Sarraj.

In *al Lama* (Shining), Abu Nasr Sarraj, known as "The Peacock of the Poor" in the eleventh century, describes seven paths and ten trances of the Sufi. The stages of the path are attained by fulfilling the requirements whereas the levels of the trances, the inner feelings, are more difficult to reach since feelings are harder to control. Abu Nasr Sarraj names the following stages: *Pledge, Honesty, Giving, Poverty, Patience, Obedience* and *Satisfaction.*

In most Sufi writings the stages and trances are described in stories where the novice Sufi (salak) travels through mountains, valleys and meadows, encountering obstacles, for example menacing creatures of true or imaginary natures. Only devoted salaks with strong hearts who do not get discouraged by these obstacles in their way are able to complete the journey. Attar uses allegory, a conference of birds, to relate a journey of a salak:

> For the cause, they ventured the trip;
> in endeavor they became clever and swift.
> Convincingly agreed and said,
> need someone with resolution and wit.
> A leader able to guide us on the way;
> his orders, we pledge to obey.
> A Master with vision to foresee,
> to guide us across this immense sea.
> (Attar, M. T., 1596)

Here the birds are asking for a leader to guide them across the "immense sea," which stands for the completion of the Sufi training.

> The world is a talisman, with treasures in its depths, yet,
> the talisman will be removed, along with the body chains.
> As the talisman is gone, you will find the treasures
> as the body is gone, the life appears.
> Then, another talisman awaits your life;
> in the unseen your life is a body, a new strife.
> (Attar, M. T., 213)

The secrets of the body can be understood with worldly knowledge. The secrets of life cannot be understood unless the talisman of this world and the body are gone. Once this happens, the soul becomes like a body in another world which again cannot understand the secret of the Lord. That secret is known to the Lord only.

> So many have befallen in this path;
> the one in trance knows this fact.
> Everything is possible in this path;
> faith, sympathy, despair, and deceit,
> but, the essence of the secret cannot be told;
> we cannot steal what we cannot hold.
> You hear these from the heart and soul,
> not from the body made from clay-soil.
> Now the battle of body and heart is intense;

sing melancholy, our affliction is immense.
(Attar, M. T, 1589)

T
he path of the Sufi is not an easy path. Many have failed trying to attain it.

Choose, as I have, this distinct way,
deep in the sea of the austerity.
In the depth with patience remain lull,
then you will find that precious jewel.
(Attar , M. T., 112)

The way of Sufi is to have proper thoughts and patience and a stern body.
These characteristics will help the Sufi student to attain the Sufi goals, here metaphorically referred to as "jewels."

As philosophically we have been told,
the scenery of the unseen world,
the philosopher expresses their point of view,
the critics discuss whatever is new.
A conservative disagrees with both;
the hypocrite is exhaustively at work.
Some in honesty reveal their way,
to show they are truly on the trail.
Know this fact that not all are true;
nor they are totally lost in the blue.
Since the truth will not come from false,
by the scent of gold, the fools give their hearts.
If abundant cash were not around,
hearts could not be so easily swapped.
In the absence of truth there are lies,
for the glow of truth the lie shines.
They buy the wrong hoping it is right,
exchange sugar with poison at their sight.
So long as there is sweet tasting wheat,
the sly traders of barley will benefit.
Claim not all religions are stories and lies;
the scent of truth lures the renegades' hearts.
Claim not all are hypocrisies and thoughts,
the truth creates fantasies in our minds.
Truth is in the holy night and other nights;
only the test will tell the nature of a night.
O' friend, not all nights are the holy night,
nor devoid of truth are all other nights.
Among the cloaked men choose one;
with the test see if he is the one.
But who is around to know this test?
To separate the errs from au fait.
If there are no damaged goods,

the merchants would be the fools.
With no defective goods, the experts are fools,

since easily can tell the quality of goods.
Also will be no profits, with imperfect goods;
will have no orpin if they are all ordinary wood.
He, who claims his way is right, is mislead;
he, who says all are false, has a hard head.
The merchants of the Prophets are with gain;
the merchants of scents are bruised in pain.
The eyes of the treasures shows the serpent;
open your eyes, and see what seems pleasant.
Do not look at the profit in trades,
recall the Pharaohs and his aids.
Look at the beauty of the turning sky,
the Lord has said relay on your sight.
Do not become content only with a glance;
look repeatedly, your vision will enhance.
(Rumi, II, 2923-2947)

Rumi discusses the essence of Sufi philosophy and points out its differences in comparison to Greek philosophy. He also notes that most cultures and traditions possess part of the Truth in their beliefs and that only by looking at all of them can we begin to glimpse an idea of the entire concept.

Peir

The attainment of the stages would be impossible without the guidance of the *peir*, i.e., the "guide," or "leader." In Sufi philosophy, all prophets are known as *peir*. The name is also used to refers to those whose faith, piety and ascetic ways lead them to the realization of the eternal Truth.

The birds told Hoopoe: by your wit,
tell us how to undertake this trip.
This position of mastery and guide,
would not be fitting those weak in heart.
The Master said; in these times,
those in love do not think of their lives.
As you put up your life for this faith,
orthodox and others are treated the same.
Enemy of your lives came as your hearts,
the end is here so free your lives.
Your lives are obstacles, let them go;
leave your sight, so you see the road.
If you're asked to abandon this and that,
you should abandon what you were asked.

If a nay-man says in his book this is banned,
tell him love is beyond this or that.
Love is apart from blasphemy and faith,
the path of love is not a concern in lovers' faith.
The lovers will set the barns aflame,
they punish themselves, for the blame.
Pain and hardship are fitting for love;
tales of love is hardship and blood.
O' friends pour my blood in that cup,
if I cannot give enough, borrow some.
Love needs the pain that closes the eyes,
the pain that entraps lives.
A speckle of love is better than all,
a speckle of pain is better than love.
Love has come as the creature of brain,
but love is never without the pain.
The angels have the love but no pain;
for only human is honored to have the pain.
The one ardent in the way of love,
will pass beyond faith and Islam.
Love will open the gates of poverty,
then poverty will open blasphemy.
As you exhaust the faith and blasphemy,
you see your life and body are gone away.
Then from this you will become a fit man,
fitting for the secret of the path.
Come forth in here as a brave man,
fearless of the blasphemy of the path.
(Attar, M.T, 1163)

Attar here discusses the novice's path towards Sufism. He tells the novice that he needs to trust his intuition and be willing to face the burdens and pain of a path that is hard to follow.

In each circle stands a leader
testing us goes on forever.
The good natured will excel
those weak in heart will fail.
The Living Saint is our Leader,
his blood line is of no concern in here.
He is the Leader and the Guide,
in absence, presence and other times.
His Gabriel is his wit, his guide;
he is the leader and bears the light.
Our gathering is lit by that light,
should know there are levels of lights.
The lights of truth are in seven hundred veils;
layers and layers of veils of lights in queues.
Groups by their orders behind the veils;

standing behind their guides in queues.
The last queues from their own weakness,
cannot see the light for their lack of endurance.
The front queues, for the weakness of their sight,
cannot stand the glare of the coming light.
(Rumi, II, 815)

Rumi gives an explanation of various religions. The "Living Saint" refers to the Sufi leader. His guiding light appears to the Sufi student as the angel Gabriel appears to the prophet Mohammed. Rumi insists that a Sufi must have perseverance and patience to achieve incarnation with the Lord.

Without the guidance of your Peir,
the journey becomes of malice with deceit.
A traveled and familiar road,
without protection you will apprehend.
But for an untraveled road
follow your leader, behold.
If you don't follow the leader and cheat
ghouls with spells will take you in deceit.
Ghouls will drift you and harm you quick.
this has befallen to those who were swift.
Listen to the Prophet in the story of those,
who had befallen to Satan in these roads.
They were taken away a thousand years,
were cheated, stripped and left in tears.

Those who went with no Guide on these ways
with deceit of ghouls ended in wells.
Do not follow the wishes of your lust
follow your guide to the road of God.
(Rumi, I, 2943)

In the following story Rumi explains the connection between a Sufi and God. He presents two lovers, one of them says, "'I have died from myself and I am alive only from you and I have lost my own traits and have taken your traits, I have forgotten my knowledge and have inspired your knowledge, I have lost my strength and move from your strength and if I love myself it is because I love you.'"

A beloved asked a lover in a test
in the morning as she called his name.
"Whom do you love more, yourself or me?
explain this truly I want to see."
Answered: "In you I vanished in a way,
that nothing remains in my empty shell.
Nothing remains from me but a name;

nothing is in me, except your name.
In such a way I vanished in you,
that in the air vanishes a drop of dew.
As a rock transforms to a precious gem,
the old quality will change to that of the sun.
The quality of the rock will no longer be there,
the quality of the sun will be from end to end.
Then, if the gem falls in love with itself,
it is the love of the sun, O' friend.
And if a gem loves itself to the end,
undoubtedly it is the love of the self.
Whether the gem loves itself,
or whether it loves the sun,
cannot tell apart these loves,
since both are the love of the sun.
The love of the rock is for joining the sun,
this love in the rock creates the inner fight.
The rock is the dark and sun is the light;
to the end will last this inner fight."
(Rumi, V, 2020)

Venture to lose the traits of rock
to transmute to have the traits of the sun.
In your venture and agonies be patient;
so you see in you the life in the naught.
(Rumi, V, 2038)
The bird is high in the air in flight,
but its shadow aground on the run.
The shadow is what the fools hunt,
'till they themselves are run aground.
Unaware that the game is above,
they search for it on the ground.
As they shoot towards the shadow,
in vain only they loose the arrows.
The quivers of their lives become empty,
in chasing the shadow unknowingly.
The shadow of the Lord is a guide,
that baffles our thoughts and minds.
The creatures are from the shadow of the Lord;
only God is alive, others are dead to this world.
Hold on to him now and have no care,
you will escape the malice of the justice day.
The story of the shadow is for the Saints to say,
the shine of the sun enlightens their way.
Venture not these roads without a purpose,
without my leader, the Sun of Tabriz.
(Rumi, I, 417)

The Sufi believe that the physical world is *unreal* whereas *the other world* is the real world.

> Qhoutb is the lion and his work is to hunt;
> other creatures eat what he leaves behind.
> Endeavor your best in pleasing him;
> so he becomes swift in hunting the game.
> The creatures will starve, if he is hurt;
> the alms of the brain is this loaf of bread.
> Since the creatures nourish from his hunt,
> remember, if this is the wish of your heart.
> Creatures are the bodies and the brain is the center
> the brain determine the movement of the members.
> Weakness of the center is in the body, not in the heart
> weakness was not in Noah, but in the ark.
> Center is the one that revolves about itself;
> it is where about which the heavens turn.

> Aid him in the ark with repairs,
> If you are one of the believers.
> You will gain more than him from your aid.
> The Koran quotes "those who aid us, we will aid.
> *(Rumi, V, 2339)*

Rumi compares the center to a leader of Sufi novices. "Qhoutb" is inspired to convey the Lord's strength, compassion and forgiveness. Attar quotes Jonid of Baghdad in reference to the idea of a leader's guidance, "...a man by the name of Nasari planned a pilgrimage to Mecca. On his trip he visited Jonid. Jonid asked him of his ancestry. Nasari replied, 'I am from Gilan and I am from the line of Saint Ali. Jonid said, 'Ali had two swords-one to fight the heathens and the other to fight the desires of within. From which blade are you?' Nasai thanked God for having guided him to the house of Jonid and said that here was his Mecca... (*T. O.*, 510)."

Inner Self

The *inner self* is not a stage but the source of many of our actions. Sufi masters state that the "self" is of evil nature and is constantly seeking sensual pleasures and lust. The self, Satan, and the desire for the temporal world all may contribute to a Sufi student's deviation from the ways of Sufi. In order to control the desires of this "self" special training is required.

Hajviri, in *Kashfu'l Majhoub*, quotes Tatsari: "The training of the novice is based on resistance and abstinence,...abstinence and resistance work against the inner self, and unless the inner self is known, abstinence and resistance are useless...."

O Lord we killed in battle the foes we saw;
now we are facing the foe of inside.
It is beyond our strength to kill this beast,
for fighting the lion, a hare is unfit.
The self is a hell, a dragon, the blazing beast,
stronger than the might of the seven seas.
Even if devours the seven seas,
his desire to destroy will not cease.
Infidel fighters with the hearts of stones,
fear of facing him, rattles their bones.
Calm will not come to him by abundant food;
but can be tamed by the call of truth.
Never is pleased, never content;
it ventures only to burn and hurt.
Devours the world and still in search,
to please his unending urge.
The truth comes suddenly to its surprise
then he retreats to lair inside.
The self is a hell from the big hell apart;
has the trait of the big hell in its heart.
To kill the beast must use the heavy bow,
the might of truth and straight arrow.
Only straight arrows fit this bow
the crocked are rejects and laid low.
The true ones will be received by the bow,
the pure are true and they easily go.
I returned from the battles of outside foes,
to face the inner foe I need that bow.
"In victory we battled we went far."
Now with the Prophet, "I face a bigger war".
I want the strength of truth to open the seas;
I want to bring the mountains to my knees .
The Knight can break the lines of foes
but the Champion can kill the inner foe.
(Rumi, I, 1373)

To have control of the desires of the "self" is more difficult than breaking through lines of armed knights.

The Self is a dragon asleep, but not dead,
with the right weapon will leave the bed.
With the weapon of Pharaoh in his hand,
chases Moses from the sea to the river bank.
The one yearning the weapons of the Pharaohs,
forces many Moses off the righteous roads.
The dragon remain dormant in the cold;
with the right tools a fly is a hawk, bold.

69

Leave the dragon in the cold asleep.
Keep him off the sun or the warm wind.
If he is sleeping or down, he is tame;
as he wakes up, you are his game.
Unless you check first, you are check mate;
act now with no mercy or it is too late.
As the hot sun brings out the lust,
the inner bat will venture out.
Venture a holy war and kill him fast
you will see your freedom at last.
This work is not for an ordinary man
we need a Moses for this task.
(Rumi, III, 1053)

Rumi refers to the story of a snake catcher who brought a dormant dragon to Baghdad thinking that it was dead. But the dragon, after being exposed to the warm sun of Baghdad, became active and devoured the catcher. Clearly, the dragon is a metaphor for the inner self, and, as Rumi writes, "we need a Moses for this task," implying that we alone cannot conquer our inner selves but need guidance.

Vow

Sohr-Verdi, in *Avaref al Ma'aref*, writes: "Vow for a commoner is repenting and promising to the Lord for not repeating a sin, and for the chosen (Sufi) it is awakening from neglect." They asked Sousi: "What does vow mean?" He said: "It is refrain from whatever the Knowledge has reproached and (to follow) whatever the Knowledge had praised."

Regarding the *vow* for not sinning, Attar, in a story of a leader who had sinned, writes:

With a vow sincerely uttered,
a world of sins will be cleared.
The waves of His sea of kindness,
will clear everyone's sins.
(Attar, M. T., 1511)

Rumi, in his story titled "A lover who wrote love letters and recounted the favors he had done for his love which the mistress did not like...," notes:

However you stay eager
as one who is thirsty at the sight of water.
The dry lips are the testimony,
as who reaches the water of the reservoir.
The dry lips have a message from water
which ends the anxiety and wander.
The dream is a venture so blessed
it removes the obstacles to the faith.

This dream is the key to your desires,
it is your triumphing banner.
The dream of the Harold who at the dawn,
reporting the coming of the sun.
Desire, though you have no tools,
none is needed on the path of truth.
If you see one with demands
follow him and become his friend.
So you learn from him to demand,
and in you the dream becomes dominant.
(Rumi III, 1439)

Do not stay idle without the dream,
or your hope will not see the gleam
the seeker will finally find
for the seeker is the ardent one.
Swiftly work with an open mind,
rectitude is blessed by God.
(Rumi, III, 37: 8)

Abstinence and Asceticism

Sohr-Verdi in *A.M* writes, "For abstinence the prophet had said: whenever you see a person who has chosen abstinence, attend to him for he is the owner of knowledge (184)." During the abstinence and stage of asceticism the novice learns about the morality of the way of the Sufi. When the novice takes the vow, he will follow the guidance of his leader to achieve this stage. Once he recognizes the right deeds from the wrong and learns to refrain from the deeds which are considered outside of the Sufi way, he is considered to be on the right path. In this state, a Sufi will earn the vision of recognizing the benevolent action from the questionable ones.

Attar in *K. M.*, quoting Bashar Hafi, writes "Abstinence means that you recognize your good deeds and calculate your deeds for each blink of the eyes... Devotion is the kingdom that does not fit anywhere except in the heart...it means...being generous in destitution, honest in solitude and expressing yourself in the presence of the one you fear (164)."

Quoting Yahya Mazad Razi, Attar writes "Varaa (abstinence) is gaining the knowledge without paraphrasing, and this abstinence is of two kinds, the abstinence that dose not fit outwardly except for the Lord, and there is another abstinence from within which will come to your heart from the Lord...and Zohd (asceticism) is setting aside the ornaments, bodily pleasures and the temporal world...from asceticism grows generosity to the kingdom and from kindness generosity to the body and the soul...asceticism is more willing to leave the world than to desire it...Devoted person on the surface is who appears pure on the surface but complex within but the Sufi is who in appearance is complex and pure within (438)."

Quoting Ahmad ebn Asem al Antaki, Attar in *T. O.* writes "There are four signs of asceticism: (1) believing in the Lord, (2) avoidance of the crowd, (3) devotion to the Lord, (4) not committing an unjust act [under the shield of] the holiness of religion (484)."

> Who in certainty is devout,
> will let go of the world and beyond.
> Only the truth will be in his heart,
> his place in heaven is close to God.
> *(Attar, P. N., 324)*

Quoting Abu Bak'r Shebli, Attar in *T. O.* writes: "...devotion is carelessness since this world is a small place and devotion to a small thing is inadvertence...devotion is to forget the world and not to think of eternity...[devotion] is nothing, since whatever your desire will finally reach you, ...and whatever you do not desire will never reach you despite your effort to devote [your time] to those things that will be yours [rather than] those that will not be yours (719)."

Quoting Fosiel Ayaz, Attar in *T. O.* writes "...the Zohd (devotion) is to be satisfied with whatever is given by the Lord and whatever He does with his creatures since the best people who are content with the Lord's givings are the Sufi (121)."

Poverty

In *Pand Nameh* Attar advises:

> O friend, be frugal in your life,
> nothing is as bitter as indigence.
> *(Attar, P.N., 379)*

Believing that our actions are in the hand of the Lord, the Sufi learns to control his emotions and thus his life becomes simpler. This teaching makes the Sufi learn not to be angry if the events do not turn to his expectations. Some Sufi writers have considered *poverty* as a separate religion by itself due to its importance. Attar also quotes Ebrahiem Adham of Khorasan who discusses loneliness and the difficulties of attaining poverty:

> One complained of his loneliness,
> also fussed over his Dervishness.
> Blessed Adham told him O' friend,
> was poverty level easily attained?
> *(Attar, M.T., 2621)*

Attar explains, "Three principles are associated with poverty: independence of the heart, simplicity of the account, and inner peace; and three things are required for the wealthy: pain of the body, complexity of thoughts and difficulty of the accounts (T.O., 283)."

> Be mindful of poverty O' friend

if unaware, to this you must attend.
The man of poverty in destitute pretends,
in riches and wealth he is well assured.
He is content when in need,
to foes, he is a friend indeed.
Though his hands are empty, his heart is full,
for this he shines with dignity to our rules.
Though weak and lean he may seem
his devotion is as strong as it can be.
Join me my friend along the Sufi road,
then you will be seen by the Lord.
Ask not for help at times of woes,
no one except the Lord will do.
If you become a friend to the poor men,

you become an intimate in Heaven.
(Attar, P N, 379)

On the same subject Ghashiri in *R. G.* writes: "Ebrahiem Adham said we chose the way of the dervish and we became wealthy and those who went after riches became destitute (455)." Sore-verdi in *A. M.* writes: "Nuri said: 'The poor [the person who attained poverty] is happy even though he achieves nothing and is humble if he achieves something (185).'"

If you want to lose yourself to the Sufi way
cleanse your heart from lust and desire.
What you have in your hand, give away,
and have smile if malice comes your way.
(Jami, Divan)

Whoever earns the hat of poverty,
will open the gates of secrecy.
This hat will not be easily gained;
the one with the hat, has lost his head.
As Attar, place your soul on this road;
you will be given the hat by the Lord.
(Attar, Heilaj Nameh, 314)

Attar states the importance of the level of poverty since from this level other levels are attained.

Rumi in the story of "a man advising his wife not to belittle the poor and look at the masterpiece work of the Lord rather than being scornful towards the poor for their opinions and thoughts and the supposition of their poverty," writes,

Riches of gold is a hat for the head,
that protects the one with no hair.
But the one with attractive tress,

with no hat, would look the best.
The man of truth is with the light,
better naked than covered from sight.
At the time of auction of slaves,
the healthy ones will be undressed.
But sellers would not uncover the sick,
many faults are covered in deceit.
If the seller is asked to uncover the slave,
would say: from shyness he will run away.
For a man with faults, but with means,
a cover may be provided to please.
But the one under the spell of greed,
is blinded to his faults and his deeds.
The assay by the beggar at the corner,
values none in the trading house of jewelers.
The work of the Sufi is not easily grasped
ridicule not what you do not understand.
Their work is of a special kind,
for the Lord guides them with His light.
The pay of Sufi is not of money of gold,
it comes from the treasures of the Lord.
The Lord is merciful and most kind
to the Sufi in love He will be also kind.
Some receive the rewards and are blessed
others are punished and are burned.
Fire will burn the one with unkind thoughts,
of the Creator of this world and beyond.
Poverty is glory in elegance, from beyond,
no, is a thousand honors of the hidden kind.
(Rumi, I, 2343)

Poverty sublimely came to dignity,
so I leave the greed to become wealthy.
The treasures are hidden in ruins to show,
that the greedy's values are placed low.
(Rumi, V, 716)

Patience

Poverty is the prerequisite of *patience* and a person in poverty without patience
will never reach poverty nor any other stage. Shor-Veri in *A. M.* writes: "It is said:
Every being has an essence, the essence (of the deeds) of human is his brain, and the
essence of the brain is patience; knowledge and patience belong together the same way
that the body and soul, the elevation of the soul depends on patience and knowledge
(184)." Because of the importance of this stage many believe that patience is a faith in
itself or at least half of the faith.

The glow of the Lord emanates patience,
the poison from Satan creates the haste.
The fear of poverty is the work of Satan,
which closes the gates of patience to you.
(Rumi, V, 58)

O' Dear in this revolving world
be patient, be frugal but not bold.
With patience remain in place,
no plan with trivia enlaced.
The learned for our guidance did state,
in all places patience is praised.
Errors are the fruits of haste
Follow what the learned embraced.
(Attar, Asrar Nameh, 113, 158)

Ghashiri in *R. G* writes: "In dervishy there are four elements: knowledge that keeps him, honesty that keeps him away from certain things, certainty that overwhelms him, and remembrance that makes him accustomed to the way (459)."

Be humble and take the silence's gold,
with patience go along the road.
Then comes to you the patience's fruits,
the golden key that opens the gates.
Think of the Lord with patience,
so you find Him in your essence.
(Attar, Asrar Nameh, 113 &181)

To refine the pure from the grounds,
how long must labor our minds.
The tests of winters, the test of falls
the heat of summers, the springs like life.
The clouds, the thunders, the rains, the winds,
are here to display the variations in things.
And the khaki color earth to expose
what is hidden beneath in gems and spoils.
Whatever earth has stolen and covered with soil,
of the sea of kindness, the treasures of the Lord.
The constable of destiny is after the truth;
asks the earth for the list of stolen goods.
The corrupt earth will deny its deeds;
destiny tightens the shackles on its feet.

In this the constable becomes kind and sweet,
and at times becomes harsh and mean.
The thief finally confesses amidst,
the hope and fear, it surrenders the list.
Spring comes as the grandeur of the Lord
fall is His threat and forgiveness, behold.
Winter is the four walls of the jail of truth,
so the corrupt ones abide by the rule.
Time is needed for a worrier's spirit to boost,
and pain of anguish and deceit to sooth.
Our body is made of water and soil,
which tries to steal the lights of our souls.
The cold, the heat, the pains from the Lord,
is placed on us, O brave friend behold.
The fear, the hunger and our bodily faults,
are the exchange for the price of our lives.
The promises, the threats and fantasies
are for mixing of the pure with lees.
As the truth and false are mixed in one,
the soul and matter are mixed in one.
You must choose and abide by these rules,
for in these are found the test of truth.
So for the treasons to be exposed
These prudent rules are imposed.
(Rumi, II, 2950)

Rumi describes our hardship on earth, i.e., away from the Lord. Our bodies, referred to metaphorically as the earth in this verse, try to cover and tarnish our souls. But destiny uncovers our souls and reveals the good and bad in the soul.

Obedience

No better explanation of the essence of obedience can be found in Ghashiri's *R.G.*, "...obedience is having a handle on the plans of the self and the man has attained obedience when he knows that the Lord is aware of the ongoing events as well as the thoughts (249)." Quoting Abu Nasr al Seraj, Ghashiri writes: "The condition of having attained obedience is that you submerged yourself in the sea of believing and having complete trust in the Lord while being satisfied with whatever is given. If the Lord gives you, thank him and if the Lord takes it away, have patience (249)."

The man who in God has no trust
his future will be lost in the dust.
(Attar, P.N., 279)

Said Noah to infidels that I am not me;
I died from a life, and was born to this.

Now only the truths I feel and see,
as the temporal senses died in me.
Now this talk is of else, for I am not me,
to this only the infidel's claim is contrary.
(Rumi, I, 3124)

The one after the riddle's reason,
the land of lost is his destination.
As he settled in this lonely place,
only reason loving beasts he will face.
As from those notions he is cleansed;
Leave their books only to the fiends.
(Rumi, VI, 1192)

Stayed in the midst, lonely, not helped,
in the dark as the faith's caravan left.
Grab on to him and hold on tight,
for He has you always at his sight.
Or you will not raise as the Messiah
nor will sink in the earth as Koran.
As you are removed away from here,
gone, but for you he will be there.
(Rumi, III, 344)

Break the jug, go to the streams;
set the temporal things, senses aflame.
Be no bandit in the pious road,
worship nothing but the Lord.
(Rumi, V, 4081)

The lover searches for the One
that its beginning and end is one.
(Rumi, III, 1418)

Rumi, in the story of the conversation between a Sufi and a judge, writes:

The Sufi Asks the Questions
When the gold is extracted from the same mine,
bring profit or loss at different times?
When the children are born all the same,
why is one sloth, another with brain?
Since the origin of water is the same,
why is bitter in swamp, sweet in stream?
Since the same sun starts each morn,
why is one bliss, the other brings mourn?
Since the wine is poured from the same jug,

why does one remain sober, other becomes high?
Since the Lord has said the pious way is mine,
why do some become bandits, the others guides?
Since oneness was seen by only a few,
why does ebullition come to many anew?

The Judge Answers

The judge said, "O' Sufi do not be amazed,
regarding these saga hear these tales.
The doubts of the lovers in their love,
are caused from the certainty of the above.
As the Lord is tranquil in his ways,
the lovers are agitated in theirs.
His smile brought misery to many,
much rues came from his dignity.
The reasons for the why's of the wrong,
stems from the sea of no reasons for why's.
(Rumi, VI, 1603)
The dyeing pot of the Lord works in a way,
the stained ones entering are dyed the same.
As the pieces enter to remove the stains,
joyously they say: your orders we obey.
To claim "the Truth," is removing the stains,
as the iron changes to the color of flames.
The trait of iron vanishes to that of the blaze,
the iron becomes proud, though no has flames.
As its rusty color to yellow is changed,
now the iron is elated, proud of its traits.
From the essence of fire and color of flames,
in joy the iron says: I am fire, I am ablaze.
It says, I am fire and if you doubt to such,
for a test come forth and touch.
Fire I am and if convinced you are not,
place your face here and feel how hot.
The one enlightened by the light of the Lord
the angels will bow to his threshold.
He needs not to bow to other men;
for he has passed the tests, amen.
Fire, iron or other metaphors used,
were not written to be ridiculed.
Either do not enter this sea and talk less
or stay by its shore in silence.
Though not many have my endurance,
nor the courage to take the chance.
My life, my wit I will throw to its feet
the price of my blood is paid by this sea.
I will as long as my feet will carry me,

to be drowned in this immense sea.
(Rumi, II, 1345)

Do not close the mouth of this pot ;
this pure pot deserves no cover of mud.
O' keeper of secrets, tell us some tales,
what did the falcon bring in today.
From afar I sense a mystical fragrance;
the one came from Yemen to Ahmad.
Mohammad said the westward winds,
from Yemen carried the aroma of the King.
This for Ramien was the soul of Vais.
the aroma of the Lord from Ovais.
The aroma of unknown of Gharan or Ovais,
placed the Prophet into the path to trace.
The Cardamom soaked a while in sugar,
will no longer have its taste of bitter.
But Cardamom coming from me and mine
it is cardamom with the taste of brine.
(Rumi, IV, 1824)

The pot of one color of our Christ
wins over the other coloring pots.
This world came as a desert of salt,
whatever enters soon will be lost.
The men of colors on this earth,
will lose their colors at end.
This salt desert of this world,
servers the desert of the other world.
The desert of knowledge the desert of truth,
whatever goes there becomes anew.
(Rumi, R.T., 1855)

Rumi notes that Sufi follow no "color," and anyone can join.

It is your father's share to have you as a son;
It is someone else's to have another for a son.
It is someone's share to be brute and mean.
It is for another to be kind and sweet.
By a hundred thousand names He is called,
He is the glory but to praising blind.
The trusted friend who seeks fame,
like you, he is despondently disarrayed.
Why do you adhere to a name,
rigidly, you stay still to the end?
Follow the virtues, forget the name;
the virtues that lead you to the way.
The discord in men is caused by names,

follow the virtue and peace will prevail.
A gentleman gave a coin to four lads
all of different tongues of different lands.
A Persian, a Romano, an Arab and a Turk
all craved grapes but unaware of the words.
The Persian said we should all agree
to buy "Angour" which is good for me.
The Arab said "la" by the will of Allah
I want "anab" which is good for a fellow.
The Turk said hear me you "afandi"
I want "ozom" looking good, as you see.
The Romano said "estroughouri" I need,
I know they are tasty and have no seed.
They raised their voices to the level of shout,
from ignorance of their neighbor's tongues.
(Rumi, II, 3675)

Rumi discusses the fact that the Lord does not need us to tell him of His greatness. He also speaks of linguistic difficulties between cultures. "Angour," "Anab," "Ozom," and "Estroughouri" all mean "grapes" in their respective languages.

Learn from the great Prophet of the Jews,
in search of truth what he planned to do.
With such a sublime level in Prophecy,
he sought the way of Love and fantasy.
Moses set his book and ways aside,
to seek the truth from the other side.
The gallant Key Quobad as he rode,
proudly to venture the unknown.
Moses, knew his and aware of these,
O' Sky how long will you search this sea?
Moses said: "Enough and reproach less,
follow the sun and the moon a little less.
I will go to the place of the joining seas;
so by the Owner of the Time I am seen."
(Rumi, III, 1962)

Rumi here indicates that Moses was also a Sufi at heart, though he was a great prophet of the Jews.

Saint Love recked the ship for the wooden piece,
to meander through the narrow passes with ease.
Since only the small ones pass, break your pride,
join poverty and let it be your guide.
(Rumi, IV, 2756)

In the Sufi tradition, great emphasis is placed on becoming a humble person and considering oneself a "small" person. Rumi uses the broken pieces of the ship as a metaphor to show that smallness is to be prefered over being large and glorious.

The essence of colors is no color
as peace is the cause for wars.
The other world is real and this is a chain,
as joining is the essence of separation.
Why are we so opposing, O' friend,
why are so many created by the Lord?
As the speckles, life and body, are gone
the battle becomes the battle of the sun.
(Rumi, VI, 59)

To join various groups which do not follow the correct path will cause dis-
agreement. This happens only in *this* world, whereas in the *other* world these matters do
not exist.

Thence, you reach the valley of oneness,
the abode of solitude and prudence.
The faces that pass through this abode,
they came from the same void.
As they appear in numbers many or few
only one number appears to your view.
Since one in Constancy is always one,
that one in one is always a complete one,
that one is not one; but a singular one,
that in numbers appears to you as one.
Since this of singularity and number is apart,

keep away from the finish and the start.
The start is gone and eternity is the finish,
how could naught stay amidst of either one?
Since all are nothing and naught is all
could these twisted riddles ever be solved?
(Attar, M. T., 3694)

Attar here describes the earth as the "void," and presents a play on words
involving numbers and measurements of the physical world which will disappear in the
other world.

The modest sees the beauty in qualities
the one with qualities is lost in essence.
The chosen are overwhelmed with essence,
how could they observe His qualities?
If your head is submerged in a ravine
how could you see your reflection in the stream?

If you come in the color of water from abyss
your woolen wrap will be shedding fibers.
The sin of the chosen, the obedience of the mass,
the joining of the mass is from peculiar veils.
If the king asks for the chancellor's account,
the king is a foe and no longer a guide.
If the account of the chancellor was false,
then the act of the king would be just.
Had the chancellor accounted to himself first,
he was the first judge to determine his fate.
(Rumi, II, 2812)

At first, one might be confused by observing the abundance of the Lord's creation, but later one will be overwhelmed by His greatness. However, if one is concerned with only one aspect of life, one will be preoccupied and will not see other aspects of life which are the Lord's manifest.

The following lines appear as the conclusion to the story about a man who chased a thief who had just left the man's house. As the good man was about to catch up with the thief, another thief saw his friend in danger of being caught, so he called for help saying, "My family is in danger." The good man stopped chasing the thief and went to answer the call for help from the second thief. When he reached the second thief told him, "... I know in which direction the thief fled." The good man replied, "I almost had him before you stopped me. You must either be very stupid or you are a thief yourself."

In what the second thief considered to be the right behavior (saving a fellow thief from being caught) and in what the good man thought to be the right action (putting others' well-being before ones own) we encounter different points of views: what is considered sin by one party may be seen as benevolence by another. In this case the chosen's sin is identical with the right act of the thieves. It takes a special act to make thieves do the right thing, i.e., join the way of truth. It takes special means to convince the masses, which include the thieves and others with non-conforming traits, to join the way of the Lord.

Satisfaction

Sufi are not in agreement about whether "reza" (satisfaction) is a stage or a trance. Attar in *T. O.* quotes Zoul Founoun Mesri: "...and said: Reza means to be happy despite of bitter events...Reza is submission to the happening events, and not being bitter from the events, and befriending in the mishaps....(188)."

Do not be scornful from the events,
in predestined, be obliged and content.
(Attar, Asrar Nameh, 99)

The Sufi student will learn to cherish everything that is God given as a blessing. Once he has learned this, he will attain the stage of satisfaction.

Sufi is the son of now, O' friend
talk of tomorrow is not their faith.
(Rumi, I, 134)

This stage will remove any anxiety that an aspiring Sufi might have and will cause him to have a pleasant disposition and an optimistic view of life which will result in happiness.

Hear of the good travelers in these tales,
they have no complaint from events.
They are chosen, apart from those who pray,
at times they sew and at times they tear.
Harken the tales of another group,
who sealed their lips from prayer for good.
Travel through the events tranquil and content,
it is forbidden to wish to change the events.
They feel the joy, the benevolence in news,
the Lord gave them that beautiful point of view.
It is forbidden to ask for an event, diverse,
need no grieves, no black for no remorse.
(Rumi, III, 1878)

Rumi explains the joy in realizing that everything, whether appearing good or bad to the human eye, is godgiven.

Once a Sufi was asked by a man,
"Tell me how you feel if you can."
Said the Sufi, "The One forever great,
His will causes the happening of events-
flow of water in the rivers to the seas
orbiting of suns, meteor's paths of speed,
destiny of his champions, the faith of lives
are by His wishes, through their time.
He sends afflictions to where He wants,
to others, well wishes, and happy thoughts.
At His will a novice joins the Sufi path;
also others on other paths ending in traps.
Without him, no lips will show a smile
without the will of the Owner of Time."

Hearken that the major event
will not happen without his hand.
As the events become pleasing to a man
His will become the volition of that man,
without pains, claims and rewards,
The man is honored to have such heart.
he won't desire his life for his own,
nor will he seek the lust of the world.

In places of orders and ways,
the life and death are the same.
He goes after the Lord, not for his gains
he dies for the Lord, not for the fear of pain.
His faith is for the wanting him,
not for the promised garden of Eden.
His desertion and sacrilege is for the truth,
and not from the fear of firing blaze.
This came directly from His source,
without ascetic anguish and search.
Why should such a man complain or pray?
since the Lord controls our events.
Why should he utter prayers, unless
pleasing the Lord he sees in his pray.
(Rumi, III, 1905)

Rumi points out that love has to be unconditional and can only lead to the love of the Lord.

Take this prodigy from me O' friend
with your share from the Lord be content.
These thoughts will make you witty and alert,
prepared for a sudden unfortunate event.
While others from their worries faint,
you will smile as a merchant in gains.
No rose is sad by losing her petals,
nor will she abandon her delightful smile.
She has no worries from falling aground,
for she had given pleasure to the crowd.
(Rumi, III, 3259)

Section IV:
Songs of the Heavens

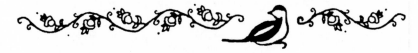

Songs of the Heavens are the trances that a Sufi may experience. Trances are inner feelings of ecstasy that are purely individual. Thus, they may or may not be experienced. Sa'di in *Golestan* writes: "One of the good *peir* of Lebanon, whose greatness was legendary in the land of the Arabs, came to Damascus. At the edge of a water-hole he slipped and he fell in. He struggled hard to get out but finally hoisted himself out of the water. After finishing his prayer, one of the followers said to the peir, "I am amazed and would like to ask you something." [The peir] told him to ask his question. [The follower] said, "I remember when you crossed the West Sea your feet did not get wet. But why did you almost die in this small water-hole?" The peir began to think about the question and after pondering for a while replied:

> One asked a dervish who lost his son,
> "With your great knowledge and vision,
> from Egypt you sensed the scent of the shirt,
> why did you not locate your son in the well?"
>
> Said: "That like a thunder is our Trance,
> at times is with us and at times none existence.
> At times, high above the horizon is my seat
> at times I do not see in front of my feet.
> If the dervish stayed in his Trance
> he could shake the two worlds' hands."
> (Sa'di, Golestan, 24)

Trances are inner exercises and contain a certain order, i.e., one needs to attain one trance after another. There are also interior stages which influence inner feelings, but various writers do not acknowledged these stages. Seraj's divisions, for example, contains the following trances: *Vigilance, Intimacy, Love and Kindness, Yearning, Hope and Fear, Confidence, Utterance, Observance, Disappearance, Assembly, Certainty,* and *Gnosis.*

Vigilance

A Sufi should be vigilant in his actions and thoughts to stop undesirable thoughts from entering his mind. *Vigilance* is described in the Orfani dictionary as: [a] perpetuation of the realization of the follower to the knowledge of the Lord to all aspects of him."

In *T. O.* Attar writes "It is said [Jonind] had a follower whom he prefered over the others. The other followers grew jealous. When the master became aware of their jealousy he told them: "'His manner and understanding are better than those of others.' [They] replied: 'We have [different] views. Let us take a test....' So [the master] had them bring twenty birds and advised them: 'Every [one] should take one bird and take it to a place where no one can see you [and then] kill it and bring it back.' All left and killed the birds and brought them back except for the master's favorite who came back with his bird still alive. The master asked him why did not kill the bird. He replied: '[You] said to take it to a place where nobody can see me but everywhere I went the Lord could see me...(509).'"

In the fourth book of *Masnavi* Rumi writes:

> When you are vigilant and aware
> every moment you hear his answer.
> If you are vigilant and hold on to the rein,
> you will see the reward before the judgement day.
> The one who knows the spell well, then
> he has no use for clear instruction.
> Your retardant brings you mishaps,
> for the spell and riddle you did not grasp.
> If your heart is darkened by the wrong,
> be aware but do not wait too long.
> Or else the missile of dark will become strong,
> and delivers it to you for waiting too long.
> It is for the forgiveness that the missile does not hit,
> and not for the reason of you not being fit.
> As you heart wishes be quick and vigilant.
> then each time you gain a gift, new and different.
> If you work hard with ambitions,
> you will reach the sky by your vigilance.
> (Rumi, IV, 2461)

Intimacy

Intimacy (ghorb) is described in the Orfani dictionary as the "elevation of the vehicles between the worshiped and the rejoicer."

Attar writes:

> As the flames of love engulfed intimacy,
> from it was born a jubilant butterfly.
> Grasping a moment of intimacy,
> is the pleasure of a dew that joins the sea.
> The dew that joined the sea,
> the image of the beloved will see.
> *(Attar, M.N., 235)*

In "The exegesis of the news of the statement of Saint Mostafa regarding Ali Younes son of Mati" Rumi writes:

> Said the Prophet that in my climb,
> did not use the ladder of Jacob.
> His has rungs and mine has wheels
> O limitless is the Lord's intimacies.
> Up or down is not the way to His intimacy;
> reaching is being free from the frame of entity.
> Naught needs no place of high nor low;
> there, the time does not run fast or slow.
> The truths treasures are in naught 's workshop
> if proud of existence, aware he is not.
> Some are happy by breaking things to waste,
> as we enjoy winning money with our good fate.
> Tools of no tools is what He cuts;
> to be in oblivion is an honor with heights.
> *(Rumi, III, 4512)*

The prophet Mohammed's ascencion to gain the the Lord's intimacy is compared to Jonas staying in the belly of the whale and Jacob climbing the ladder.

Love and Kindness

Love and Kindness (mohabbat) is one of the best and most important trances of the Sufi. Sohr-Verdi in *AM* writes: "The master said that the prophet begged for the special love and should know that love has many faces and comes in many kinds: first, the love in the soul, then love in the heart, then, the love in the mind and then the love in the essence (188)."

One of Attar's poems on the subject reads:

> If your eyes are open to see love
> you become jubilant and forward.

(Attar, M.T., 1078)

Her love brought my faith and doubts,
it is a flaming fire in my heart.
If I have no one in my sorrow,
for me is enough to confide in love.
Love made me to bathe in my tears,
from the veil I was banished by the tress.
(Attar, M. T., 2228)

Attar quotes Jonied: "And said: Affection is entrusted from the Lord.... And said: Affection will not become real between two persons unless one calls the other "me." And said: As affection becomes real, protocol will no longer exist. And said: The Lord has forbidden affection for the man in (illicit) desires. And said: Affection is indulgence in reaching the desire. And said: You will not reach the affection of the Lord without exposing your body to hardship in his way *(T.O. 519)*."

Rumi writes:

From Him comes the lovers jubilance and grieves,
also the services and the rewards of their deeds.
If other than the Beloved you seek,
your love is untrue, a dream, a fantasy.
Love is the fire that once it comes with flames,
except for Beloved all will burn.
The killing sword did not unjustly cut;
see what is left after the work of naught.
All will be gone except for the Lord of above;
now rejoice, the blazing Love.
Since he was the first and will be last
see dualism only in viewing of events.
It is surprisingly pleasing , vis-a-vis,
without life no movement is made by the body.
The life that causes void in the body;
it will not be sweetened even if dipped in honey.
He who had lived once knows this for fact,
sipped the wine's soul from the soul's hand.
To the one has not seen the face of Beloved,
the life is nothing but heat and vapor.
The one who has not seen the generosity of the Saint,
will assume the Haji's action is the best.
He who saw in the snake of Moses no stability,
will assume life is in ropes and sorcery.
The bird that knows of no water fresh and sweet,
will rejoice in the salt water of the sea.
Since the like cannot be known from its unlike;
how can the melody be recognized from a strike.
But first was created the world,
so you appreciate the value of the land of the Lord.

90

As you are released from here, you will go there
in the eternal confectionery you will become a worker.
You will say there I was sieving the soil.
and ran away from this pure world.
Before this we were in the naught,
had less pain than we had in the mud.
(Rumi, V, 586)

Rumi states that the "like" can be known by its "opposite," as days can be
known from the nights; however, the being of the Lord cannot be known from our existence.

In "The Story of Saint Aziz" Rumi writes,

The sons of Saint Aziz were out,
the news of their father they sought.
The sons but not the father had grown old;
the father suddenly appeared on the road.
The unaware son said: Hey lad,
do you have any news from our Dad?
We were told after long that today,
our father will come back by this way.
Aziz replied: After me he will come soon.
The son fell in joy as he heard the news.
The son cried and uttered the news loud,
the older son from the sight of the father passed out.
Then he said, Why are you happy from the news
since we have fallen in center of fortunes?
Hope is for thoughts but the brain is after the fact,
the one with vision for hope does not lack.
The infidel with pains and the pious with hope,
but the one in love is for the present and cash.
The one in Love is for now and the loot,
no doubt, he is above the faith and doubt.
Faith and doubt are the keepers of his gates
faith and doubt are the covers for the brain.
Doubts have formed the layers of dry,
faith has formed the layers of joy.
The dry layers are suited for flames;
the layers of enjoyment is connected to brains.
The brain itself is better than joy;
it is better than relish for it enjoys.
(Rumi, IV, 3271)

In the story of "The Test of Lokman in which Lokman was used as a food
taster; whatever food was brought to Master was tasted by Lokman, and if Lokman ate
the food then the Master would eat. Once some bitter melon was brought to Lokman,
who ate it with zeal and once the Master tasted he found it to be bitter" Rumi states:

Someone sent the Master a melon;
for testing, the Master called Lokman.
The melon was cut into pieces;
for testing to see if they were safe and sweet.
Lokman ate, the pieces given to him;
the testing went on till he ate the seventh piece.
Lokman ate the pieces so eagerly,
that others crave the melon avidly.
As the Master placed the bitter in his mouth,
burning sensation came to him at once.
Then he was sickened for a while,
as he controlled himself, called Lokman.
Asked, "How much bitter can you eat?
How many favors for hostilities can you return?"
Replied, "The blessing I received from your hand,
which I am thankful for and cannot pay back.
I was ashamed for the bitter you gave,
for your kindness, this bitter I will bear."
"If from this bitter I should complain,
in all places myself, I will belittling."
Kindness will make sweet from bitter;
kindness will make gold from copper.
Coarse becomes smooth by kindness;
pain becomes pleasure by kindness.
Kindness will make the dead alive;
kindness will makes slaves lords.
Kindness is knowledge by itself
how could fallacy have such zeal.
(Rumi, II, 1514)

Hope and Fear

Fear (khouf) is defined as "one of the stages of the path, the fear of the death of the beloved, and the entrance of an unwanted into the heart."

Ghashiri in *R.G.* writes "Junied said that for whoever is afraid of anything except the Lord, all doors will be closed and fear will come to him and will be covered with seventy veils (46)." He continues, "Hope is giving your heart to a friend that you are as well accepted, the same way that fear belongs to the heart, the enjoyment of the heart is in need of hope; there is a difference between hope and begging, since begging will cause indolence...(198)." And: "Fear and hope are the two wings that will be used to fly through space to be close to the truth (199)."

Saleh said: Unless the heart has not experienced fear, it will not reach love and kindness (186)."

Attar in *T.O.* writes, "Abu Solieman quoted Saleh Abdul Kariem saying that fear and hope are two lights in the heart and was then asked which one is brighter. He said hope. He was further asked what the meaning of this was. Why would the light of hope be brighter? He replied, 'Do I fear the Lord that his punishment is the fire, or do I fear the Lord that his end result is the fire (331)?'"

In a story entitled, "Since the pretender does not know the opposite of the truth, he will not know the truth either, but since he acts in sincerity his misunderstanding is forgivable," Rumi writes:

> The fear of pious of the judgement day,
> is for the account of his sins and obeys.
> But, the Sufi planned on this from the start,
> to make himself free from this account.
> At first he had his fear and hope
> but, he learned to get rid of both.
> The seasoned farmer that has planted vetch,
> knows the work of the harvest and storage.
> As Sufi studied the work of these two,
> the riddle was shortened by the blade of truth.
> His fear and hope were for the Lord;
> the fear was gone and remained only the hope.
> (Rumi, V, 4065)

Hope is characteristic for people who expect something desirable from the future. However, Sufi do not expect anything in return and believe that the Lord should be worshiped because of his greatness rather than out of fear for the judgement day.

> The Saints have told us not to despair.
> There is no limit to the Lord's grace.
> From his benevolence do not despair,
> hold on with his mercifulness reign.
> Impossible plans, difficult schemes,
> then with ease the solution will be seen.
> The wonderful hope will follow despair,
> the light of the sun makes the darkness disappear.
> (Rumi, III, 2923)

Yearning and Intimacy

The Orfani dictionary defines *yearning* (shogh) as "the struggle of the heart to see the beloved" and *intimacy* as "the enjoyment of the heart from the beauty of expansion of love toward the beloved."

Quoting Fares, Ghaishri in *Resalat* writes, "Fares said that hearts with yearning are enlightened with the light of the Lord, and as their yearning moves, it will enlighten the space between the earth and the heavens. The Lord will present them to the angels and will tell them that these yearn for me and I yearn for them even more (577)."

Attar explains:

O' Lord, by these tales you gave me abilities,
like a butterfly I have the urge avidity.
If I drink from your sea of eagerness;
my yearning will make me to be in ebullience.
My desire made me to came to this land,
with the same spirit I will return to the pure world.
Your desire makes me brag as in the coffin I lay,
and will proudly rise for the judgement day.
If all my body becomes hearing ears,
the music of your name will make me unconscious.
If all my body becomes sound.
I will echo you only your name.
If all my body becomes eyes,
they will seek you only behind the secret veils.
If a speckle is left from me or none,
I will know and call you or no one.
(Attar, A.N., 111)

Confidence

Confidence, (etminan) which leads toward tranquility, is the result of having complete faith in events. This trance could also be called ethbat (confirmation) which is defined in the Orfani dictionary as "proof of finalizing the truth in naught of the traits of man."

Attar calls the opposite of confidence "the valley of perplexity." He describes what a novice lacking *confidence* will face.

Then he reaches the valley of perplexity
will labor with pains and envy.
With each breath the pain of a cut
each moment, the moment of doubt.
The sigh of the burning pains
the nights and days that never end.
The blood from the root of each hair
writes of the pain and despair.
The dormant body with the inner blaze
the freezing with ice, the burning pain.
The baffled man as he reaches there
looses the path for he is not aware.
Even the mark of the unity of the Lord,
will disappear by its discord.
If he is asked of his state of trance,
or of his naught or of his existence;
or asked if he is in the middle or out,
or he is to either side or not,
or asked if he is a mortal, eternal or both,

or if he is in existence or in naught.
Will say just do not know what I am;
that too I know not if I am.
In love I am but do not know with who;
do not know if I am a Moslem or a Jew.
But of my own love I am not aware;
my heart is full but emptiness is there.
(Attar, MT, 3801)

Hafez describes *confidence* and the lack of it.

For my beloved I have thanks, and I have wails;
the faithful of love, should listen to these tales.
I rendered my service but not for pay nor for bind;
O' Lord, hope no one has workers with no grace.
No one has offered drinks to those thirsty thugs;
seems no longer our friends live in this lonely place.
I will not leave your door, though you brought me
shames,
harshness from friends is better than favors from the
foes.
The trap, the lock of her tress, O' heart do not fall;
or you will see, by the bend, for no crimes severed
heads.
We are in blood, the beauty of your eyes have made us
so;
it is unfair, O' Dear, to aid the killer of the loving hearts.
In this dark of my night, I have lost my chosen path;
O' guiding star, show yourself from the covering clouds.
Whichever way I faced, nothing but the fear came,
beware of this desolate land with its endless roads.
O' sun of the chosen ones, I am boiling from heat
inside,
set me, for just a while, under the shade of grace.
The end of this endless road, cannot be known to us;

for it begins at first by thousands of miles of roads.
Your love will end with cry, if you act like Hafez;
recite Koran by heart along with its fourteen tales.
(Hafez, Divan, Ode #94)

Hafez discusses the problems inherent in this stage. He relates that there will
be both satisfaction and complaints when one is on "the path of love."

In the "Story of the Rivalry Between the Chinese and the Romans" Rumi tells
us:

Chinese painters said we are the best
the Romans said we are no less.
The King said without a test,
cannot really say who is the best.
Of the rules and conditions they talked,
from talking the Romans paused.
The Chinese agreed on the needed space,
the Romans settled for an equal place.
There were two houses in symmetries;
one for the Romans, the other, the Chinese.
The Chinese asked for many colors of paints;
the king opened the treasury for the test.
Each morning from the treasures of paints,
the Chinese asked for different shades.
The Romans asked for no tools nor paints;
wanted to remove the residue and wastes.
They polished the walls behind the doors;
with purity of heavens with no other work.
Whatever glows behind the clouds,
are from the moon and the stars.
As the Chinese finished their work;
happily, they played the music of joy.
The king came and saw their design,
amazed at the beauty, wonders of mind.
Then to the house of Romans he looked,
for this the curtains were removed.
The reflection of the Chinese murals,
also came from the Romans' walls.
The Romans reflected with their walls,
the beauties of the work of other side.
Those Romans of clarity are Sufi in heart;
free of rhetoric, books and arts.
Their hearts are polished, cleansed of dust,
free of misery, envy, and lust.
That polished mirror undoubtedly is the heart,
fitting to reflect the beauties of all.
The faceless face of eternity, unseen,
in mirror is what Moses had seen.
The eternal face will not fit in the seas,
nor in this world, nor the sky, we see.
For all these are with limits and ends;
unlike the heart, with no limits nor end.
Now here in silence the mind is lost,
for it is with the heart or is it the heart?
The reflection of faceless forever will glow,
the eternal face, through our hearts we know.
The polished ones are free of colors and arts,
they see readily the beauty in their hearts .

(Rumi I, 3467-3494)

Attar describes the stage of *confidence.*

> After that, it will come to show,
> the veil of Knowledge without a head, or toes.
> No one exists in this place,
> from the various paths, so diverse.
> Here, each path is unlike another;
> the Sufi of the body, the Sufi of the spirit is another.
> Again, the body, the life, deficient or sublime,
> always in advance or decline.
> Thus the many paths that comes to show,
> each to its limits will come forth.
> How can one becomes a patriarch in this path?
> The travels of the falcons, the speed of the ants,
> the travel of each is set by his limits, defined
> the intimacy by one's desires to the sublime.
> As a little fly takes off with its might,
> turbulence of the air will be light.
> But as various paths, so many so diverse,
> no two manners can possibly be the same.
> Knowledge came to us in different ways;
> some bow to the east, others kneel to alters.
> As the sun of knowledge begins to shine,
> from the heavens, the path of sublime,
> each man to his own limits will see,
> the extent of the truth to his degree.
> Now the secrets of the speckles are revealed;
> the furnace of the world, a flower bed will be.
> (Attar, MT, 3477-3489)

In the first story of *Mathnavi* and in "The Reed" Rumi writes:

> As the flowers vanish and the garden is gone,
> the nightingale no longer sings their tales in songs.
> All are from Beloved, the lover is a veil;
> only Beloved is alive, the lover is dead.
> If the love for Him has no cares:
> pitiful is the case of a wingless bird.
> How do I think of here and there,
> impossible with no light from the Friend.
> Love is eager to reveal these words,
> but the dull mirror, he is confused.
> Do you know why your mirror shines not?
> Its face is dull from the dust.
> (Rumi, I, 28)

Expressed here is the Sufi essence: to believe that only the Lord is alive and all comes from Him. The mirror of the heart is the only way through which we can envision the Lord. Hafez in the following ode uses the *challis of Jamshied* as a metaphor for the mirror of the heart:

> For years my heart yearned the challis of Jamshied,
> what it already had was demanding from me.
> The pearl that was away from the mother shell
> asked directions from those lost by the bay.
> Last night to the Peir of Magi I took my puzzles,
> who had the visions to solve the riddles.
> Saw him content, with the challis in his hand,
> he saw many visions even of far away land.
> I asked, "When were you given the challis of Jam?"
> He said, "At the time of making of the blue heaven."
> Broken hearted he was, but the Lord was with him.
> Not knowing, he was performing for Him.
> The magic work that was performed there,
> was the same work Moses did with a cane.
> The friend who made the Gallows holy by his touch
> was hanged for the guilt of revealing the secret.
> If the Holy Spirit give us a chance once more
> what Jesus did could be done by others.
> I asked the use of the beloved's wavy tress;
> replied: "The cry of the broken heart of Hafez."
> (Hafez, Divan, Ode #140)

The *challis of Jamshied* ("Jamshied" refers to an Iranian king during the Kiani dynasty) stands for the enlightened heart which has the power of vision. The *challis* was said to have magical power and reveal all secrets.

Utterance

Utterance (zekr) is the Sufi way of meditation in which the name of the Lord is uttered in repetition. The Sufi utter the name of the Lord in their gathering, some in unison, others in chanting, for meditation and to enhance their concentration.

Ghazali in *Kimial Saadat* in the ninth Asl writes "Zekr appears in four kinds. The first is the one on the tongue where the heart is unaware. Although it is weak it is not empty since a the tongue that is busy in serving is better than a tongue which is idle or waiting. The second kind is in the heart. It is imperative to force the heart not to return to its usual way of negligence. The third kind is the one that resides in the heart and one must force the heart to do other chores. The fourth kind is the predominant kind in the heart. It is the effect of the Lord over the heart of the caller and not the utterance...(370)."

Rumi describes this stage as follows:

We said so much, imagine the rest,
if your thoughts are still, go and rehearse.
Rehearsal invigorates the thoughts,
rehearsing for the depressed is the light in the dark.
The essence fascinates, but behold O' friend;
beware of fascination, go on and work.
Leaving your work is a pleasant thought;
but it calls for total sacrifice.
(Rumi, VI, 1475)

Rumi writes about the message the Lord gave to Moses:

Said to Moses, On Me you should lean,
call Me with the mouth that you did not sin.
Said Moses, But I know not of such mouth,
Replied, Then call Me with the others mouths.
through others mouths that you did not sin?
Then through those mouths call Me.
Do your deeds such that those other mouths,
praises you through the days and nights.
Through those mouths that you did not sinned,
are the mouths of others, since you concede.
If you cleanse your mouth of the passed sins,
you will be enlightened and quicken your wits.
Utter the name of the pure, and once it comes
the ills will surface and soon will depart.
The adversaries runs away from foes
as the light comes the darkness will go.
As the holy is called by His pure name,
ills and sorrows will no longer remain."
(Rumi, III, 180)

Rumi also relates the story of a person who was in *utterance* but received no response.

A man was uttering the name of the Lord at nights
so from that, sweetness would come to his mouth.
One night the Satan came to him and said:
"You uttered much but no answer was returned.
no answer will come from his threshold,
with your utterance, why are you so bold?"
This broke the man's heart and laid low,
then he dreamed of Saint Love in a meadow.
The Saint said: "From utterance you came to halt;
are you saddened for uttering of the name of God?"
The man replied, "I have uttered so long
I am afraid of rejection of my call."

Said: "Your utterance is our reply,
your pain and love is our true call.
Your resolutions and clever deeds
gave us the reason to give you the lead.
Your fear of love is the lasso of our courtesy
in each of your utterance is our silent reply.
The soul of the ignorant is away from praise
his is not ordered to utter and pray.
His lips are locked so his mouth is shut;
so he could not beg at the time of hurt."
(Rumi, III, 189)

Observance

The Orfani dictionary explains *observance* as "audience of the Lord and his observance (moshahedeh) for the reason of oneness which is above manifestation just as the level of togetherness." All stages and trances mentioned earlier are for attainment of this trance. *Observance* is also referred to as "enlightenment," "attraction," "total recall" and "oblivion." This trance is similar to the feeling of a person who travelled through mountains, streams, rivers, valleys and oceans for days before he finds his destination. At this time, he will be overwhelmed by the site of his destination and will close his eyes and sigh. In "Tardiness of the Horizon" Rumi writes:

Eye of senses is the horse and the light of truth, the rider,
without the rider the horse is of no use.
So train your horse not to follow the ill habits
or it won't pass the test for the parade of the King.
The eyes of horse follows the eyes of the King;
its eyes will be lost without the eyes of the King.
Wherever you lead the horse to its eyes,
is the same except for the water and grass,
The light of the truth rides the light of senses
thus the soul yearns the audience of the truth.
The horse with no rider knows no manners of the road;
needs a King to know the way to the Kings' roads.
Go towards the senses for it is the rider's light
the senses owns that benevolent light.
By the light of truth decorates the light of senses,
this is the meaning of the light from above.
The light of senses will lead you to the Venus,
the light of truth will lead you to heavens
(Rumi, II, 1285-1295)

Hafez observes:

Last night from sorrows I was saved;
by the fountain of youth I was placed.
Exposed to the light of the Lord, in trance,
the wine of truth improved my existence.
What a blessed time a jubilant night
the blessed and gifted in the holy night!
Now to the reflecting mirror I will face.
where I am exposed to the news of the friend.
What of it, if I was rewarded with gifts,
I was deserving to be granted my wish.
The herald announced the coming of my rewards;
my sufferings and pains for my bearing and patience.
The honey and sweets in these words,
are the gifts from the sweet bearing trees.
The fervor of Hafez and the early risers,
is their savor from the sorrows of their times.
(Hafez, Divan, Ode #197)

Disappearance

The Orfani dictionary defines *disappearance* (fana) as a "disappearance of the created in truth and disappearance of his/her inclination toward human and disappearance toward the Lord; the fall of the gathered qualities."

Attar writes of disappearance:

If only a hair is left from your being,
I will call you unfaithful all the way.
If you step out of your shell,
into the real world you find the way.
(Attar, MT, 668)

Attar also relates this story:

An old woman went to the court of Bu-Ali
offered gold pieces and said, "This is from me."
The Amir said, "I also have plights, as you see,
I can take only what rightfully belongs to me."
The woman said, "But your vision, O Great,
cannot see what is just since you squint.
Into the oblivion the man cannot see;
since there is no Mecca nor a monastery."
There will be good and bad so long as here you stay,
once you are naught, good and bad become fantasy.
If in your shell still you remain,
you will see the good and bad again.
From nowhere you who have come,

also trapped in shell you have become.
I wish you were with your basal traits;
before becoming a being, you had to wait.
From bad traits you should be freed;
so you join naught as the dust in the wind.
(Attar, MT, 3707)

Attar describes the ultimate *disappearance*.

As long as you live within the passing world,
how could you walk to the house of the Lord?
How can I walk within the house of oblivion,
so long as I am with my essence,
since not this road nor that will last?
What is the use if you learn this at the end?
The endeared seed nourished with love and care;
raised to be witty with so much knowledge and traits,
to the hands of oblivion he was given after all;
at the end, from heights, he was made to fall.
Disappear now so the truth appears in you;
reality will not come, when your living is in you.
Unless you disappear low in nonexistence,
you will not be accepted by the great existence.
(Attar, M.T., 4278)

Rumi describes this trance by referring to the story of the Roman ambassador who came to see Khalief Omar.

A messenger from Caesar travelled far,
to reach Medina, the land of Omar.
He asked for the palace, Omar's abode;
so he would take the gifts and unload.
The Medinian replied, "Omar has no palace;
but the light of his life of no palace is less.
Though he is a leader with fame, but
as a modest dervish he lives in a hut.
His palace you will see if you are keen,
then you would have seen the palaces, unseen.
Whoever has a heart pure and cleansed,
soon will see holy places and the Saints.
Ahmad was cleansed from the fire and smoke
wherever he went saw the face of Lord."
(Rumi, I, 1391)

Rumi writes:

A lover to his beloved for his needs,
was counting his services and his deeds.

Said: "For you I have done this and that
in battles I was hurt by lances and shot at.
Now my fortune, energy and fame are gone;
my time with no love was wasted and gone.
Never rose in the morning leisurely in delight;
never slept in a descent place at night."
Whatever he had tasted in bitter and pain,
to the beloved, in details, explained.
His talk was not from complaining,
but from honesty was his telling.
A hint is enough for the curiosity of the wise;
but the thirst of the lover would not be satisfied.
So he repeated his words without fatigue;
how could one stop the rain in the spring.
He was saying hundred words from the old pain
saying, "I am not saying these to complain."
He had the inner fire but did not know;
his tears like the burning candle in flow.
Beloved said, "I know you had done these acts;
but now listen good to these facts.
The real work that counts you didn't do,
the minor work you did are lost in blue."
The lover said: "Tell me the work that counts."
Beloved said: "To die and joining naught.
You did all that work but you didn't die;
die now and you would gain the real life."
(Rumi, IV, 1242)

To die is living the ordinary life and joining life is to join oblivion.

Gathering

Gathering (sama) is described in the Orfani dictionary as: "A song that uproots
a novice's feeling and connects him." The novice will not pay attention to the principles
and see nothing but the Lord. Sufi believe that music and songs help to reach trances.

Regarding Tatsari Attar writes: "It is said that when Tatsari heard a sama such
happiness came to him that for twenty five days he remained in that state and did not
eat.... When he was asked about his trance, he replied: 'Do not ask me. Neither form my
words nor form me you will have any benefits (*T.O.* 365).'" Sufi considered *gathering*
food for the soul and tranquility for the heart and considered music a sign from the
heavens. Attar writes:

Sama is a great essence in our path,
the one who heard it knows this fact.
Without the desire in your heart,
its purpose will hide from your eyes.

The one dormant to its affects,
is not blessed with the needed talents.
Desire is the foundation for love;
the one, who has the gift, knows all.
The one untouched by its affects,

will never know its real intents.
He is excused from learning the truth.
will not stand in the Sufi queues.
(Attar, P.N., 328)

This is Sa'di's description of *gathering*.

If you are for love, be less into other affairs;
or else, go after your health with care.
Do not avoid kindness for it makes you earthly;
other ways may prove to be deadly.
The sweet fruits will not grow on trees,
unless the tree gain the trance from the breeze.
The chant brings the truth closer to you to see;
helps you to rid of yourself and become free.
The way cannot be found by being sober;
those who lost themselves are aware.
To the gifted the rhythms of the hoofs of mules,
is the music of the reeds and the lutes.
No pests towards the one in trance will fly,
for he is unlike the others who passes by.
He will not know the high notes from lows,
but to him is music the noise of water in flow.
In adoring the wine, they whirl,
they become high by the noise of a wheel.
They dance and whirl as wheels,
as the screech of wheels they cry with their shrills,
in obey their heads tucked low in their shirts;
if unbearable, they tear their shirts.
Do not ridicule those dervishes in dance,
for they are overwhelmed in the trance.
O' brother, I will not talk of the Gathering,
unless I know who is listening.
If Sama's meaning is measured in height,
the angels cannot reach there in their flight.
If a man comes to Sama with lust,
his desires become robust.
If a man of lust comes to heed,
he will not gain the trance, but will fall asleep.

The violets will vanish by the seasonal breeze,
but needs an ax to remove the dead trees.
(Sa'di, Boostan, 278-279)

Gathering by itself is not a trance but a measure to reach other trances such as fana (disappearance) as described in the above story. Sama refers to the Sufi gathering during which Sufi masters give speeches and music, singing and dancing takes place. It is said that Rumi used to consider all noises around him as music, the noise of the wheel turning, the singing of the birds, the water falls and even the hammering of the carpenters. These often rhythmic noises put him in a state of trance and he began to dance wherever he was.

To the Sufi the calls of animals and other creatures mean their understanding and their way of praising the Lord.

As Adham, scatter the realm of the state,
then find the garden of Eden with its shade.
The king in his throne asleep at ease,
the guards on the roof tops to question and seize.
The aim of the king for assigning the guards,
was not to rid of the thieves and the rogues.
He always knew he was just and kind,
free from the events with clear mind.
Justice protects the wishes with its guards,
not with the mere scarecrows on the walls.
His purpose from the strums of sitar,
the lover's desire for a sign when afar.
The threat of drums and the moan of oboe
are a little of the music from above.
The philosophers had said all these songs
had come to us from the revolving stars.
It is the call of the turning spheres,
the melodies we hum with our peers.
Faithful believe the heavenly affect
changes jangled sounds pleasantly perfect.
We were parts of Adam in our past,
and heard those melodies in the chants.
Though doubts came to us by this sad land,
we still have a little of our glorious past.
But since we mixed with this afflicted soil,
the melodies do not give us the heavenly joy.
As a stream is polluted with waste,
its water will not have the original taste.
The body contains a little of the wastes,
which pulls us to the sadness of the blaze.
The polluted water will keep its taste,
and carries the sorrow of the blaze and wastes.
Sama is the nourishment for love,

for it contains everyone's thoughts of above.
It gives life to the dormant thoughts,
they may become real by the songs.
(Rumi, IV, 726-743)

Adham was an early Sufi from Khorasan. He left his position as *amir* to follow the path of Sufism.

Certainty

The Orfani dictionary describes *certainty* (yaghien) as "the advent of the light of truth discovering humanity with the testimony of happiness and desire with condition of proof." The name of this trance implies knowledge without doubt.

Attar quotes Tatsari. "The first stage of gnosis is that a man becomes certain in his secret and gains traits which bring him peace. Thus, bad thoughts result from uncertainty (*T.O.*)."

O friend, opinion seeks certainty,
for that it struggles exceedingly.
As the knowledge is gained,
the scent of certainty will be felt.
But not so in seditious paths, O friend
mere opinion will be gained.
Knowledge seeks facts for certainty,
and certainty seeks for eternity.
In Koran seek the truth for certain, (26)
not the mere thoughts behind the curtains.
Knowledge will lead the learned to reveal;
if certain, will see the great upheaval.
The pseudo thoughts and truth will never coincide,
as hunches lead to fantasies and thoughts.
In the pages of Koran find the right path,
certainty leads to having the eye of certain. (27)
I am above thoughts and certainty,
my head does not turn by profanity.
(Rumi, III, 4118)

Gnosis

Ta'rifat defines *gnosis* (ma'refat) as "knowing the affairs. Unlike science, [for Sufi] the acquired knowledge is for the uninformed, but the Lord is knowledgeable and not learned."

A learned Sufi is defined in the Orfani dictionary as "A person who the Lord has given the level of observance and audience to His qualities." Attaining this level of knowledge is the main purpose of the Sufi. In order to possess this knowledge we have to use four parts of our being: the heart, the soul, the self and the mind. The soul is the eternal part and it acts through the heart. The self is the temporal part of the human. The heart is used for understanding rather than feeling. The mind is used for acquiring the knowledge of science. Prophets and saints have this insight.

> Go and leave your rosary and cloak;
> enlightened enhances your body and work.
> The Prophet Mostafa was divinely favored;
> St. Morteza by knowledge became ascertained.
> (Attar, Mazhar al A'jayeb, 281)

Rumi in "Your being and your trance should be concealed from the ignorant" writes:

> Hear the words of a learned man;
> in trance but not from the wine he drank.
> Drunk in the body, unstable on his feet,
> mocked by the children when no one to heed.
> Fell to sides, walked with sway,
> ridiculed by imbeciles along the way.
> Such was his state, the children in front,
> ignorant of his trance, his talented mind.
> People are children in the trance of God,
> no one matures till death does him apart.
> The Lord said this life is for play and joy,
> you are the children, the world is a toy.
> Play of the children, the wars of the grown,
> mindless thoughts play with the world.
> Playing with sticks, playing with swords,
> dance to the tune of the vanishing hoards.
> Riding the horses or the horses of sticks,
> this one goes fast even on inclines of steep.
> The banners of ignorance, the following crowd,
> the faithful of destruction, speaking loud.
> Wait and see the horsemen of
> they leap the skies beyond the blue.
> The leap of the souls toward the Lord,
> their exodus rattles the entire world.
> The children playing hard with joy,
> pretentious war lords, ambitious toys.
> How could pretentious faith reach the heights?
> How could the horse of sticks leap the skies?
> The vision of the heart will help your leap;
> the temporal knowledge you must heap.
> The knowledge of heart is your friend;
> the temporal knowledge you must bear.

The knowledge you carry, said the Lord
is not a knowledge, it is a load.
The knowledge not of Him is a waste
resembles the cheap dye that fades.
But as you carry your load well
you will be unloaded, free of the weight.
Carry no temporal load in your head
seek the sea of knowledge in yourself.
Seek the knowledge, the bearing horse;
to free your shoulders from the load.
How could you escape lust without his wine;
are you content with the name of the divine?
His name brings the thoughts to you,
those thoughts are the agents of view.
The visit of no agent is without a fee;
so long as there are ghouls, no roads are free.
Do you know of a name without a meaning?
Have you picked flowers by their spellings?
When you hear a name, seek what it means
look to the clouds for water, not the streams.
Venture beyond letters and names
rid yourselves from the hard heads.
As a piece iron be free of rust
clean your heart, the mirror, from the dust.
Cleanse yourself from the attributes
then see the inner beauties in you.
You will see the gnosis of the patriarch
without teachers, being chosen or books.
The Prophet said from my roots
I have my essence and my hopes.
Their souls see me with a special light.
I too see them with the same light.
(Rumi, I, 3426)

Rumi in the "The story of the rivalry of the Chinese and the Romans over the art of painting" describes the Sufi belief that the heart should be pure and clean to receive the messages from above:

Death that is feared by all,
it is looked at by them with a smile.
No one over their hearts can prevail;
harm comes to oysters and not to pearls.
Though the religious ways are set aside,
the naught and poverty they abide.
They mingle with the heavenly designs,
from that the mirror of their hearts thrive.
They have news of the heavens and beyond
or perhaps they had the audience of God.
(Rumi, I, 3495-3499)

References

al din Jondi, Moeid. "Nafhat al Roh va Tohfat al Fotoh," with assistance of Najieb Maiel Harvari. Published by Entesharat Molavi, 1362 H.S.

al Din Mohammad Molavi ebin al Housain al balkhi al Rumi, Jalal. "Kolieat Divan Shams Tabrizi." Published by Amir Kabier, 1345. H.S.

al Din Mohammad Molavi ebin al Housain al balkhi al Rumi, Jalal. "Koliat Masnavi, Book of Molana." Published by Dara alKetabeh Mir Khani.

al Din Mohammad Molavi ebin al Housain al balkhi al Rumi, Jalal "Mathnavi Manavi," based on the gathering of Reynold Nicholson, published by Amir Kabier, 1371, H.S.

al Din Sadi Shirazi, Sheikh Mosleh. "Koliat." Published by Ketabkhaneh Markazi, Khayam, Tehran.

"Algkoran Alkariem," publisher c/o No. Chatsworth Road, London NW2, 4BH.

al Jaffar ebin Josi, Abu. "Teblis Eblis." Translation by Alireza Zekavati Gharagozlu. Published by Markaz Nashr Daneshgahi, Tehran, 1368, H.S.

al Zaman Forozanfar, Badeie. "Translation of Resaleh Ghashiri." Published by Sherkat Entesharat Elmi o Farhangi, 1374. H.S.

Ansari, Ghsem. "Avaref al Maaref, Shaikh Shahab ak Din Sohrverdi." Translation by Abu Mansor ibn Abdolmomen Isfahani. Published by Sherkat Entesharat Elmi o Farhangi, 1374.

Baghli Shirazi, Shiekh Rozbehan. "Shareh Shatheiyat," with assistance from Henry Corbin. Published by Ketabkhaneh Tahori, 1374, H.S.

Fazeli, Ghader. "Farhang, Mozoaai Adab e Parsi, Mantegh al Tayr o Pand Nameh, Shaykh Farid al Din Attar Neishabor." Published by Talauh, 1374, H. S.

Fazeli, Ghader. "Farhang, Mozoaai Adab e Parsi, Mosibat Nameh o Mazhar al Ajaeb, Shaykh Farid al Din Attar Neishabori." Published by Talauh, 1374, H. S.

Fazeli, Ghader. "Farhang, Mozoaai Adab e Parsi, Asara Nameh o Heilaj Nameh, Shaykl Farid al Din Attar Neishabori." Published by Talauh, 1374, H. S.

Ghani, Ghasem. "Discussions in Affect and Thoughts of Hafez." Published by Zavar Tehran Shah Abad, 1352, H.S.

Ghazvini, Mohammad, and Ghani, Ghasen. "Divan Hafez Shiraz." Published by Anjoman Khoshnevisan, Iran, 1362, H. S.

Harvari, Housein, with Shadman, Zahra. "Sharh Ghazalhai Hafez." Volumes 1 through 4, Published by Kayhanak, 1369, H.S.

Hassan Ali Hajviri alGhaznavi, Abul. "Kashf al Majoub," copied from V. Zhokofski. Published by Tahori, 1373 H.S.

Hassan Seydan, Mohammad. "Dow Baytihai Baba Taher." Published by Talaih, 1374, H.S.

'Holy Bible." Published by Gideons International, 1978.

Majied. "Ghran," with translation and treaties. Published by Ketabforoshi Eslami.

Maleki, Housin. "Divan, Sheykh Fraid al Din Attar Nieshabori." Published by Nasher Chekameh, 1361, H.S.

Mojahed, Ahmad, and Keyaei, Mohsen "Golshan Raz, Sheihk Mahmoud Shabestari." Published by Ma and Manochehri, 1371. H.S.

Nafisy, Said. "Les Origines Du Soufisme Iranien." Published by Librarie Foroughi, Tehran, Eighth Edition 1371. H.S.

Nafisy, Said "Preface," in "Divan Shah Ne'matolah Vali,". Published by Moasseseh Entesharat Negah, 1374, H.S.

Neishabori, Attar. "Tazkarat al Oliyaa," from Nicholson's copy, with assistance of A. Tavakoli. Published by Entesharat Behzad, 1374, H.S.

Nezami Ganjehi, Hakiem. "Koliat Khamseh." Published by Amir Kabier, 1344, H.S.

Nicholson, Reynold A. "Exegesis of Mathnavu, Maanavi Molavi, vol. I-VI," translation and expansion by Hassan Lahouti. Published by Messers Luzac & Company LTD 1995, Tehran.

Nicholson, Reynold. "Introduction to Rumi with Commentary and Annotations to the Mathnavi Ma'navi." Translated, Collated, Annexed by Ovaness Ovanessian. Published by Tehran University Publications, No. 1330, 1350, H.S.

Rodwell, J. M., Jones, Allen, and the Oriental Institute, Oxford. "The Koran," translated from the Arabic.

Sadegh Goharbein, Sid. "Mantegh al Tayr, Maghamat Tayor, Shaikh Farid al Din Mohammad Attar Neishabori." Published by Sherket Entesharat Elmi o Farhangi, 1374, H. S.

Sa'di. "Koliat," assistance by Mohammadali Foroghi. Published by Nashr Arvin, 1374.

"Translation of Ghran," no name or date of publication.